Joseph Salyards

Idothea

The Divine Image

Joseph Salyards

Idothea
The Divine Image

ISBN/EAN: 9783337779702

Printed in Europe, USA, Canada, Australia, Japan

Cover: Foto ©Thomas Meinert / pixelio.de

More available books at **www.hansebooks.com**

IDOTHEA;

OR,

THE DIVINE IMAGE.

A POEM,

BY

JOSEPH SALYARDS.

Parea dinanzi a me, con l'ali aperte,
La bella image, che, nel dolce frui,
Liete faceva l'anime conserte.
DANTE.

NEW MARKET, VA.:
HENKEL, CALVERT & CO., PRINTERS.
1874.

PREFACE.

Your author, my little book, has experienced more hesitation than difficulty in preparing you for the vicissitudes of life. At last he ventures to commend you to wide communities of men and women. His own lot forbade him to try the world under as favorable auspices as he expects you to try it. He sends you now to the Pythian plain. With a smile on your face, you must gird yourself for the contest, and acquit yourself nobly. Then you must visit different lands; enter the stately mansion as well as the humble cottage; approach the young, the old, the unfortunate, the happy, the gay, the gloomy, the intelligent peasant, the eloquent statesman, lords and ladies, even the palaces of kings, wherever knowledge and virtue are seeking an abode. You have a glad, magnificent message to convey,—this wondrous Creation of mind and matter interwoven. It becomes you to feel the weight of your message and the dignity of your audience. He wishes you to seek the very best society; assured that if they cannot admire you, they may not feel disposed hastily to cut your acquaintance; and if you cannot secure their applause, your manners, at least, will not be corrupted by evil communications. In the obscurity of a private career, he has found this world an abode sufficiently pleasant; he has felt or heard but one subject of serious complaint against the intelligence of his fellow men,—that they should seek glory in the horrors of war, and blot out the footsteps of improvement almost as soon as made. He has taught you to consider this very unwise; and still he cherishes the hope that he has made you worthy of a gracious reception.

He bids you go, therefore, with his blessing; and may you share, among the orders of mankind, that felicity which he trusts you know how to promote. He has sought to purify you, as far as possible, from blemishes both literary and moral; and he believes you will make all with whom you commune, more cheerful, more hopeful, more intelligent, penetrated with a deeper reverence for whatever is divine or holy, and radiant with brighter anticipations for human destiny.

NEW MARKET, VA.,
August 1, 1874.

General Analysis.

IDOTHEA.
I. THE BEAUTY OF TRUTH.
      Idos i.—Truth in Man.
      Idos ii.—Truth in Nature.
      Idos iii.—Truth in Revelation.

IDOTHEA.
II. GOOD AND EVIL.
      Idyl i.—Eudæmonia.
      Idyl ii.—Nemesis.
      Idyl iii.—Voices of "Hilltop."
      Idyl iv.—Waif of Rosendale.
      Idyl v.—Pride and Providence.
      Idyl vi.—The Wranglers.
      Idyl vii.—Kalonimata.
      Idyl viii.—Passing Away.
      Idyl ix.—Behind the Veil.

IDOTHEA.
III. YONDER!
      Epidos i.—Uranothen.
      Epidos ii.—At Home Again.
      Epidos iii.—Uranonde.

IDOTHEA.

I.

THE BEAUTY OF TRUTH.

Καλὸν μὲν ἡ Ἀλήθεια, καὶ μόνιμον.
Plato.

MORE LIGHT!

The verge, the verge of all we know ;
New mysteries rise, old mysteries go ;
The flashes of Ithuriel's wand,
The dawn of something still beyond,—
Behind the seal, behind the seal,
Brief gleams of hidden Truth reveal,
All beauteous as the bow of heaven,
Yet snatched away as soon as given,
The spiritual within the blue,
The radiant region of the True.
I see soft fingers, pure and white,
Half draw the curtains from the Light,
Where down each immaterial groove,
New thoughts immortal live and move.
I well may deem it lovely there :—
O, when will Genius make it clear !
Whence hope looks in from shades afar,
To woo me, like a loving star ;
Where some I love have gone to find
The transports of a wider mind.

Thou dear unknown ! The breath I draw
Is warm with some mysterious awe !
Oh, lend the hand I yet shall see,
And lift me to felicity !
There once again the Muses dwell
On sunny slopes of asphodel,

And Orphic lines and leaves ideal
Shall make us realize the Real;
Shall make us see, if we can see,
The foibles of our infancy:
The blinding meteor in the haze,
Illusive formulæ of praise;
And gifts, and glories, creeds, and crimes,
The iron bands of iron times;
Our dreams of Power and Majesty,
Dim ripples on a summer sea.

E'en now the gold-tipped clouds betray
The rosy dawn of brighter day,
When men shall know and nations see
A glorious range of destiny;
When fate shall widen as we go,
The lucid sweep of mind below,
And show, without the light of suns,
The path progressive Nature runs;
When Faith shall worship something true,
With wiser, nobler deeds to do,
And give the heart and head to trace
The hopes of an immortal race.
Ye central suns! revolve, revolve,
And ripen Nature's vast resolve.

IDOTHEA.

I.

THE BEAUTY OF TRUTH.

IDOS I.—TRUTH IN MAN.

ἀδόντα δ' εἴ-
η με τοῖς ἀγαθοῖς ὁμιλεῖν.
Pindar.

BOOK I.—ANALYSIS.

INVOCATION.—TWO SPECIES OF PHENOMENA,—FORM, COLOR, SOUND; DESIRES, AFFECTIONS, THOUGHTS, VOLITIONS.—LATTER SYMBOLS TO FORMER.—DOMAIN OF REASON.—POLAR ELEMENTS.—VOICE OF REASON AND TRUTH.—AFFECTIONS OF HOME.—PROGRESS.—SUCCESSION.—FAITH, CREEDS.—PAINTING.—MUSIC.—POETRY.—ORATOR.—HISTORIAN.—PATRIOT.—LABORS OF MAN.—REPLY.—CONTRAST.—MAN'S IDEAL NOT FOUND IN MAN.

BEAUTY OF TRUTH.

Idos I.

Great Source of beauty, inspiration, love,
From life below, to seraph life above,
Maker and Lord of continent and sea,
Thy mercy hath been mindful e'en of me.
For, I have lived where Freedom, Genius, Art,
Descend from Thee and stir the human heart:
O'er all I see the Beauty of the True,
Like stars in fountains, morn in drops of dew;
I hear the voice of ancient Time rehearse
The Veda, Saga, Myth, Aonian verse,
Where man his fresh, ethereal vigor tries,
To solve the mysteries of earth and skies.
I find the future mirror'd in the past,
Thy finger mirror'd in the Fair, the Vast;
I feast with Reason, and bright gleams have shone,
Through Man and Nature, from the blue Unknown:
I lean with Faith, and treasure, line by line,
Sweet revelations from thy Book divine.
And now most thankful for the bliss unbought,
I try the maze of feeling and of thought;
I sing to man how beautiful Thou art :—
O, light and lead this inexperienced heart!

A stranger here, unconscious how, or why,
I walk the earth; I circle round the sky!—

Fair mother, Earth, why deem our dust *below?*
Thou too art heaven, if yonder worlds are so:—
In heaven I worship, though a wandering mite;
Though clay, I breathe; though dust, I see the light!
A conscious atom on thy shining breast,
I too have been the universal guest.
Where are the árchives of this rolling Fane?
Do land and sea no chronicle contain?
No scroll to tell, no record to rehearse
The dark foundations of this universe?
How first some droplet from the sea of Mind,
In strange affinity with dust combined?
Thought, feeling, will, devotion, faith, desire,
Where burn their altars, whence their sacred fire?
Sweet Hope that kens some world of purer bliss,
And Love, Oh, Love! that makes a heaven of this?
Nor these alone possess the living brain;
Remorse, distrust, despondency, and pain,
Pale Memory with her cypress and her tears,
Illusive hopes and visionary fears.

What lends each mood the wondrous power to find
Expression from the viewless stream of mind;
To mold, to swell, in robes of spirit hue,
Form, symbol, sign, infallible and true;
Smiles, blushes, tears, the glance, the frown, the sigh,
Thought on the brow, and soul within the eye?
The sound! the voice!—mysterious power to mold
A word in air, and bid that word unfold,
While listening ears imbibe the word, the sound,
And in each brain the jewel thought is found!
Strange power! that calls on pictured walls to roam
Sweet memories of some loved, relinquish'd home:

Dear faces, forms, as Art inspires the dream,
Glide through the shade, smile out upon the beam,
O'er scroll and page, in golden lines, are wrought
Fair networks of the elements of thought ;
Old sages leave their systems on the sheet ;—
I drink by drops, and every drop is sweet!
Lo! as I pierce the hills, on car of fire,
I hear the message murmur on the wire ;
Men stretch, or plunge, the cable as they please ;
Thought thrills the earth, the ocean, and the seas.
And thus I find, I feel the power to draw,
In outward form, the grace of inward law.
And shall I trace the image, hail the sign,
Nor see beyond realities divine ?
Are these but phantoms, fragments of a dream,
And none the Beauty, none the Truth they seem ?

Ye bounding couriers of delight and pain,
Which course each nerve, and stir the conscious brain!
Thou wondrous Power, whose annual visits fling
O'er wintry wilds the garniture of Spring ;
Which mold the clay, endue the dust to be
An eye of light, a heart of ecstasy,
And lead your countless worshipers to hail
The starry zenith, and the teeming vale ;
Oh! Life, Sensation, are ye too but names
Of fluid forces in material frames ?
Freed from these atoms, can ye dwell apart,
When death arrests the palpitating heart ?
Say, when ye fly, for nobler ties design'd,
And leave us naught but darken'd dust behind,
What shares the Beauty and the Truth ye bear
From weeping earth to your congenial sphere ?

Co-heir of life, light, immortality,
Come thread these dark perplexities with me;
Pressed with conflicting doubt, belief, desire,
These problems haunt us;—let our hearts inquire
Hast thou not felt some thrilling, soft reply,
When midnight stars were throbbing in the sky;
When, hither borne from regions true and fair,
Eternal Reason stirr'd the conscious air?

"Friend of the Right, adorer of the True,
Indulge no dreamy, visionary view!
Let not the world's idolatry betray
Thy heart from proven principles away,
Nor cringe, nor tremble at the haughty frown
Of proud Authority, in sable gown;
Yet, with a mild docility receive
Each word of wisdom, and that word believe.
Thou hast a soul;—why pamper slaves to try
The morning mists, when thou canst pierce the sky?
With patient, keen analysis dissect,
And all the proud, and all the false reject.
The height, abyss explore, with sacred awe,
And sound each system, theory, and law,
Nor pause till gleams intuitive be given,
To bathe thy tenets in the hues of heaven.
Feed on the light of consciousness divine,
For lo! that light of consciousness is thine.
Eternal Reason, from whose bosom now
I speak to thee, and breathe upon thy brow,
This Reason is a self-illumined sea,
That fills and lights immensity for thee,
And this Immensity,—the First, the Fair,
The Sire, the Spirit, living cause and care.

Ensphered in Him, thy deathless soul is wrought,
A radiant thought in radiant orbs of thought:
Life, sense, volition,—sphere inclosing sphere,
Till life and sense in embryon forms appear;
And thou emergest, made to see and know
The Great Unseen's apocalypse below;
This air, this light, and that ethereal fire,
That rends the cloud, articulates the wire!

"Explore thy soul;—it hath the power to see
Life, death, embosomed in Necessity.
Things DO exist; supreme conditions MUST;
These are eternal; those but fleeting dust;
The constants and the variables of God;
Those dwell with Truth; these vanish at his rod;
These ever subject to contingent laws;
Those fixed as space, eternity, and cause;
These may thy sense empirical disclose;
Reason alone can reach the height of those.

"One summit more in Reason's sky attain;—
Behold the endless all-embracing chain.
From infinite through finite as it goes,
Dependence links and limits these to those;
Here pause, and see from Reason's dizzy height,
This metorama down the fields of light!
A living, wise Necessity hath wrought,
In every thought, triplicity of thought;
In every Truth three elements combined,
To merge in Mind Ethereal, human mind.
And as each grain, the breeze or tempest wings,
Is ruled, embosom'd in the sum of things,
The simplest Truth, from dust and darkness given,
Is link'd to one in all the light of heaven.

"Lo! born and breathing in this atmosphere,
Thou hast an ear and thou hast power to hear:
Thou walkest forth amid the morning light,
Blest with the organ and the gift of sight;
Thy soul, a drop in Reason's boundless sea,
Is made to wander and commune with me;—
For I am Truth, pure Wisdom, primal Light;
I guard the world from intellectual night;
I make the law, intuitive, supreme,
Which from the last, suggests the first extreme,
Bid thesis and antithesis divine
Flash from their poles, and in thy breast combine.
Were there no air, no light beneath the sky,
Inert the ear, inert the torpid eye;
And joyless, thoughtless were the mind in thee,
Not found amid this intellectual sea.

The function, force; the passive soul, the power;
Contrasted poles, congenial Your and Our;
Sound, silence linked, the heaving breast inform;
Height answers depth, a calm suggests a storm;
Green earth below, above prophetic blue;
Yon rolling heavens impersonate the True;
Worlds visible reflect bright worlds unseen,
With Faith, Hope, Love to oscillate between;
Joy, grief, smiles, tears, light, darkness, death and life,
Heat, cold, maintain inevitable strife.
Through darken'd space the golden stars are shown;
Without all vice, all virtue were unknown;
No word for weak, no thought or name for strong;
Right finds existence in opposing wrong;
Good, Ill unwedded, must together fall;
They live together if they live at all;

And Conscience, stirr'd as frowns or smiles behoove,
Untaught to censure, never could approve.

"I touched his spirit, and Columbus saw
The law of contrast, and believed the law;
While thousands lined the Andalusian strand,
That priest of Ocean saw his sails expand;
Erect, serene, in view of man and God,
His trust untested, and his path untrod,
One glad conception, luminous and warm,
Beamed in his eye, and swelled his manly form;
He sees, and seeing, stands resolved to find
The morning promise of his truthful mind;
Shores, regions, hills, opposed to those in view :—
His trust was tested, and the law was true."

Thy lips are still, Erasmus, yet I hear
A voice around thee, murmuring sweet and near,
Just at the soul, yet seeming in the sky,
Sweet, soft, æolian, like a spirit's sigh!
Auspicious voice! one moment more delay;
Sweet truths, awake, are waiting for the day;
Celestial gleams of sunshine cross the mind,
But rosier tints keep struggling up behind.
Sure, heaven had sent those dulcet tones before,
Long wintry nights, within my humble door!
I hear, I feel a dear remember'd tone,
A voice I knew, and knew that voice alone.
Oh! why the fairest of this world to me,
That pale, wan form upon her bended knee?
Whence the mild grace, no more discover'd now,
The quiet language of that pensive brow?

Whence came the rapture, not to hear, but feel
The midnight murmur of her lonely wheel?

"The same, the same—thy mother's, blest and free,
For all her sweet fidelity to thee.
With thee I counsel in her voice alone,—
No longer heard by mortal ears my own.—
Those wintry nights, I loved to make thee feel
A charm symphonious with her murmuring wheel;
I cheered her toils with visions of the pure,
Where woman's love and woman's hopes endure.
And now she kindled with a smile of joy;
Now paused and gazed upon her sleeping boy.
The mother!—earthly syllable nor sound
Can swell the soul with music more profound!
The day returns,—her loving toil complete,
She hastes, she goes,—but names some morsel sweet:
Then first for thee, and in thy waiting eyes,
Did Faith and Hope, companions dear, arise.
She hastes, she comes,—both Faith and Hope are true,
And Love, translated, fills thy bosom too.
All earnest feelings owe their power to me;
I teach the language, tune the melody;
Strong pulses thrill the heart of him that hears;
Ideal lustre shines through smiles and tears.
In woman's heart my softest bed I find,
My dearest home, her fond, confiding mind;
My love to man is best reflected there;
Her mission is the robe of Truth to wear:
For Beauty is the mirror of the True;
How bright the day when all the sky is blue!
When birds are singing o'er the forest ground,
Pure, sunlit airs add sweetness to the sound.

"In woman's fame your world of men concur;
You crown Cornelia, Clelia, types of her;
Your nymph Egeria rears the sacred spire,
Your Vestal Virgins guard the vestal fire;
Your bards, your sages, charm'd with every Grace,
With every Muse that elevates the race,
Have given the source of Poesy and Fame,
An immortality in woman's name.

"Inspired by her, and she inspired by me,
The young, the fair commence the world to be.
At home, with holiest names, begins the fire;
Son, daughter, brother, sister, mother, sire;—
Congenial ties, congenial wishes, aims,
Warm, melt, refine with sympathetic flames;
From breast to breast the sweet emotions spread,
Smile answers smile, and mutual tears are shed.
Though man can see, where'er his feet may roam,
No smiles to greet him like the smiles of home,
Yet cold indeed the selfish bosom were,
To bury all its lone fruition there.
Lost were the beams that beautify the bowers,
If not reflected by the leaves and flowers,
And lost the fragrance of the blooming vales,
If heaven had shorn the pinions of the gales.
The circles widen; ray with ray entwines,
Love hails the morning, day in love declines.
The festive hour, the tournament comes round,
The champion knighted, and the ladie crown'd;
With lyre in hand, the lyric bard acclaims
Olympic, Nemean, Pythian, Ismian games;
The law within, without, the wheel of chance,
O'er wild, o'er wave, the life and light advance;

You think the foolish nations are at play,
But cities rise, and mountains melt away.

"Man bids the earth her various wealth disclose;
The hills develop, and the metal flows;
He fells, he fences, plows, and plants, and reaps;
Flocks fill the vales, his cattle climb the steeps;
The axe advances, and the forest falls;
He builds him thrones, and walks in marble halls;
His pyramids, his towers, his temples rise;
His lenses sweep the undigested skies;
He weighs the planets, counts the winged flight
Of meteor, comet, gravitation, light.
He molds to music evening air and breeze;
His argosies are over all the seas;
He takes the lightning from the clouds above,
And sends it round with messages of love;
He takes the beam of morning from the sun,
And wins a grace no Titian could have won;
He bails the bounty of a pool at hand,
And steams the gifts of Commerce round the land;
He brings the magnet from the parian mine,
And makes it guide him o'er the pathless brine;
He stereotypes the thoughts of every sage,
And hands the treasure down from age to age.
Of shale or shell his curious eye may pass,
He finds a name, a species, order, class;
Each fruit, or flower, in mountain, lake, or moor,
The living things that creep, or swim, or soar.
And still he mounts, gains fresh access of light,
Brings fresh improvement from the starry height;
Each passing age extends the field of view,—
Still wide and wider visions of the True.

Thus rise the ages, but the ages pass;
Ye grow, ye ripen, but ye fade as grass;
And yet each leaves some footprint on the plain
For man to trace, and man to tread again,
Enduring image of creative Mind,
To field, and mart, and monument consign'd;
An Indian arrow, or the Parthenon,
Ye seize and say,—So far the race hath run.
Enough for these.—The hoary heads withdraw;
A younger race may find a higher law.
The Eldest-born,—the elements—repair
From grain, and drop, from leaf, and light, and air,
And from the Plenum, viewless, undefined,
Leaps the glad Æon, darts the deathless mind.
Lo! on the vale, the hill, proceed again
A fresh supply of hand, and heart, and brain;
They toil, they feel as once their fathers felt,
Rocks rift before them, and the metals melt.
The strata forms, the forest grows for this;
No leaf is lost, no atom moves amiss.
That wandering mote is on its way to sense;
That sleeping germ shall grasp intelligence;
Creation's anthem ever must be sung,
Each grain of dust is waiting for a tongue.

" And mine the boon with joyful haste to bring
The feast of Reason, as ye learn to sing.
The light ethereal fresh upon my brow,
I fly, I come, with tuneful voice, as now,
Upon my arm a mazy wreath divine,
Of braided symbol, interwoven sign,
Of form, relation, fluid force, and law—
Your moving myriads hail the sign with awe.

The braids untwine, the genial odors flow,
And throbbing pulses feel the bliss to know.
From vale and woodland sated sense retires,
Man's spirit glows with more refined desires,
Glad to forego the breezy shade of noon,
With Summer wanderings underneath the moon,
Dahlcarlia's maidens, chanting on the hills,
And all the sweets the Hyblian bee distils.
Imagination folds her sunlit wings,
Tho' warm the beam and sweet the breeze she brings,
Her visionary temples fade away;
Adieu to Fiction;—Reason rules the day!
Lo! purer, fairer intuitions beam,
Than Fiction feigned, or Fancy strove to dream.
I speak to all.:—no arbitrary choice;—
All hear the sound, and all shall heed the voice;
Forever peals the word, the voice I give;
The dead shall hear, and all that hear shall live.
Lovers of Beauty, prophets of the True,
A charm unearthly cleaves the starry blue;
They feel again the airs of Eden blow,—
Remembered flowers, remembered sweets below;—
They see a light, beyond created light;
They hear the roar of chaos on the height;
They taste, redeemed from sin's primeval curse,
The drop that binds the crystal universe.

"Then all obedient to the sweet control,
Dissolves the mute divinity of soul;
A glad belief, a full, responsive trust,
Warms, kindles all your palpitating dust;
A gentle, sweet, involuntary thrill
Pervades the heart, illuminates the will.

Contend no more,—the wise contend no more,—
In Church or State for hoary creeds of yore;
Vain creeds that boast the sanction of a name
Upheld for pride, and oft upheld in shame,—
Pride in a list of lineal heads so long,
Shame of a world that loves to rail at wrong;
The pride of Islam and the shame of Boodh,
Maintain a servile, not a faithful brood;—
Who says his faith transcends all reason's height,
Be sure his passion circumscribes his sight.
Faith kindles, lives but on the light I lend;
Can soar no wider than my gifts extend.
Faith is reflex,—a sparkling on the wave;
False lights may shine, but one alone can save;
And naught but Reason, naught but Light divine,
Can make you know the spurious light from mine.

I am the Light, in love and mercy sent,
To cheer the darkness of your banishment.
True Faith and I, reciprocal in this,—
We cheer with proofs and promises of bliss;
Our voices swell in waves of harmony,
I sing my love, and Faith responds to me.
Ye see the sun, with delegated power,
Call out to life, and beautify the flower;
Ye see, as morning moves in light along,
How all the woodland opens into song,
And still she widens o'er the streams and isles,
The ripples laugh, the branches break in smiles;
Thus am I sent in beauty, light, and love,
The spiritual light that cometh from above;
From world to world, in living radiance brought,
I tip with glory all the heights of thought.

Then genial laws and systems rule again,
And smiling Freedom walks the happy plain.
Till Faith, enlightened, need no more disown
Sweet adumbrations dawning from the Throne.
I raise the veil before the Good, the Just,
And let their beauty warm your smiling dust;
There shine the heights your virtue must achieve;
There smiles your native home! Behold, believe!"

   Spirit of Truth! I tremble,—not with fear:
I know it is the voice of Love I hear;
This strange, voluptuous rush of thoughts unknown,
With fearful sweetness agitates mine own.
I love thee, Spirit! cannot disbelieve!—
That voice remembered would not now deceive!
From days primeval never all unheard,—
Genius in Greece; in Solyma, the Word.
O, THOU must be most beautiful and wise!
I see thee only as I see the skies!
Away! Ye lovely of the earth, away!
True, ye are lovely, but your charms decay!
Charms of mortality, no more for me,—
Ye fading fictions of felicity!
No more within the forms of shadow bound,
The Grace, the Touch triumphant, I have found.
Kneel, glad Devotion, lo! thy shrine is here,
Pure, bright, ethereal, beautiful, sincere,
Here sweet repose, fruition in the mind,
The restless wish, the burning hope may find,
Pillowed in rest and rapture on the True,
With Nature's apotheosis in view!

   "Soft, mortal, soft! Thyself a child of dust!
Revere thy brethren; love them, and be just!

Faith in the soul, and Reason in the mind,
And free their own felicity to find,
They act a part;—not all of mortal clay;
Within the jewel lives the solar ray.
Behold the lustre, in sweet lines of love,
On smiling cheek, on radiant brow above,—
Those garlands of divinity entwined
Around the temple of ethereal mind.
They act a part, and shall, with hand and brain,
One day, their forfeit Paradise regain.
Your laws of optics are no laws to me,
I look around the world's rotundity,
Through light and shade, all climes at once I view,
Spring, Summer, Autumn,—kindling, fading hue;
Forever sounds the busy hand of man;
I shape the purpose, hint, improve the plan;
Illume the thought, invigorate the will,
Add skill to labor, truthfulness to skill.
Beneath the stars, I hover o'er his dreams;
I lure, I lead him by the summer streams.
As in the shell, beside the ocean found,
Primordial fountains in his spirit sound!
That spirit kindles,—looks, and sighs, and sees
Ethereal beauties leaning from the trees.

" In ages gone, thus oft my whispers stole
Along the chambers of his listening soul;
A charm ethereal o'er his visions came,
His brow dilated, Freedom swelled his frame.
I breathed desire of something still unknown,
Refined his speech, gave music to his tone,
Displayed the azure mirror of his mind,
The world in lovely miniature designed,—

The skies, the seas, the fields, the gardens there,
And human faces more divinely fair.
The wilderness relenting to the light,
Broke into garden spots, from height to height,
And peaceful cot and consecrated dome,
And vows of love, and holy joys of home,
And sweeter smiles enhance his youthful bloom,
And tenderer tears, and memories of the tomb.
With fruits and flowers the vales began to shine,
He saw the light, and knew that light divine.
Joy, admiration, into worship grew;
His fruits he offered, and his victims slew;
With liquid tones, he cull'd me loveliest name,
And Rhea, Isis, Ceres, Vala came,
With sacred orgies through the starry night,
With service solemn and mysterious rite;
The glad enthusiast, kindling as he knelt,
The pencil seized, and fixed the charms he felt;
Through years of patient, deep devotion woo'd
Celestial Beauty from her solitude,
And o'er the canvass, in the marble wrought
Fond traceries of his dear ideal thought.

"I tuned his raptures to the Dorian mood,
In Orphic hymns that charmed the solitude;
Wild creatures hurried from their wild domain,
Around to worship, and repay the strain.
Kind heaven has woven with harmonious sound,
In generous souls, a sympathy profound;
Joy, love, devotion, courage, hope, desire,
Are chords symphonious to the tuneful lyre.
Terpander fired, Timotheus ruled the heart,
And Orpheus knew each tuneful touch of art.

But Haydn now, in varied strain sublime,
Transports the soul beyond the birth of time,
And o'er the surge of forming worlds afar,
Notes the first anthem of the morning star.
I snatched a measure from an angel's lyre,
And touched his spirit with the heavenly fire,
Her trembling chords, responsive to the thrill,
Man's proudest domes with joyful echoes fill.

"I am the Muse, invoked when poets sing;
The living thought, the deathless word I bring.
The bard whose soul is nearest the Divine,
Finds, where he wanders to commune with mine,
A shining sea, whose truthful depth reveals
Each purer ray the starry height conceals,
Where golden clouds, of golden light enwrought,
Are but the vesture of immortal thought.
Fond child of wonder ! his the joy to tell
The beauteous forms in which a thought may dwell;
How Life, and Love, and Hope, and Faith, may glow
In spirit-shapes invisible below,
His words are vestures of the bright unseen,
With golden hours, and golden hopes between;
The Infinite, the Possible, the Pure,
Where bliss is Being, and where Joys endure;
Said, but unspoken; felt, but unreveal'd;
No form discloses, as no form conceal'd.
Modes, manners, customs, morals, passions, seals,
Need revelation, and his Word reveals.
Such was the bard Mæonian, Hesiod such,
And Pindar, with his sweet, religious touch;
Such Æschylus, and tender Sophocles,
And later minstrels, musical as these.

"These are the media of my love to man;
The symbols of an undeveloped plan;—
For symbols are the autograph of God,
The sands of Eden which his feet have trod,
Your poets sing, your orators proclaim;
They both transmit, not constitute, the flame.
I breathe around a warm, intense control;
I pour the urns of wisdom on the soul.
They feel a viewless river rolling through,
Lit with the light and beauty of the True;
Their eyes with rapt astonishment expand;
They utter thoughts, and learn to understand,
Lo! there he stands, in majesty of mien,
His form erect, his shining brow serene;
His swelling height, his reaching arms embrace
The heavenly streams that flow upon his face,
His voice to moving modulation strung,
Eternal mandates burning on his tongue;
With liberal hand he sows upon the throng
The light inductions as they breathe along;
Persuasion wakens, wins the yielding breast;
The Truth, triumphant, and the people blest.

"I led my votary to the ocean wave;
I sat beside him in his lonely cave;
I bade him cull the sweet, the simple grace,
The living light of Nature's honest face;
I bade him learn the lore of every Muse,
Interpret man in all his forms and hues;
Power, principle, affection, passion, pride;
I taught him how to mold them, how to guide;
To prompt no vain, no visionary hope,
With turgid phrase, declamatory trope,

With barren point and pitiful conceit,
But watch the height where Truth and Beauty meet.
Men haste to hear him from the Attic plains,
Women of Ida, and Arcadian swains.
They lean; they drink the wisdom of his tongue,
His glory ripen'd, and the ages rung.

"That glory, fed from streams that never dry,
The grave Historian and the Sage supply.
Industrious Memory swept the ages past,
And bade the wisdom, bade the lesson last.
Far up the clouded stream of time she flew
Thence teeming fields of rich instruction drew.
Here, gray Experience weighs the shining lore,
Compares, arranges, sifts the treasure o'er;
To each event its parent cause assigns;
The end of law and government defines;
And as the glass divides the solar ray,
Sets this to virtue's, that to passion's sway.
When righteous aims the patriot's arm attend,
When Justice weeps, and Factions re-ascend,
He lifts on high the mirror of each mind,
A warning light, a beacon for mankind.
He lifts on high the virtues that combine
To rear a state, or shield it from decline;
By honest toil and independence fired,
By faith, and fame, and liberty inspired.
In all its aims and purposes sincere,
No power offended and no power to fear,
Its wealth, its arts enlighten all the land,
Its wings of Commerce o'er the seas expand;
Its rulers, men of honor, wise, serene,
Untaught to truckle, witless to be mean;

E

Wealth, splendor, power, prosperity increase,
Repose awhile in glory and in peace ;
Till luxury, intemperance, and pride,
With gradual force the towering frame elide ;
It rots, it ruins, hollow with decay,
And human glory creeps in smoke away !
Behold ! at noon the fleecy vapors rise,
Like lambs of heaven, disporting in the skies ;
One little cloud attracts the rest around ;
It spreads, it widens, darkens o'er the ground ;
The lightnings glare, the rifting thunders play,
It breaks in torrents, and dissolves away ;
Cloud parts from cloud, along the ethereal plain,
And light and beauty smile on earth again.

"Why grows an empire? Grows it but to fall ?
Ask Thales, Plato,—ask the sages all.
Why grows, declines the body of a man ?
To muse, discover, build, remodel, plan,
To live, and love, and work beneath the sun ;
The body crumbles, but the work is done.
His tomes of science, monuments of art,
Remain in Nature, and become a part.
Thou wast not born a savage in the wild ;
The sire has made a cradle for the child.
States, kingdoms, empires, organons of power,
Supply conditions potent for the hour ;
Perform the work no single hand can do,
Decline, dissolve, and leave a work for you.
Decline, dissolve, obedient to a law
Which wisdom gave, and patriot sages saw ;
For this is true philosophy, to know,
Not WHAT you see, but WHY you see it so.

Life is succession. Shall a tree ascend,
Invade the clouds, grow on, and never end?
What grows on earth, cannot forever grow;
Still change eternal is the law below.
The tides advancing hear the seas recall,
The very height precipitates the fall.
This sum of things in wondrous wisdom made,
To rise, to bloom, implies to fall, to fade.
All but the Centre moves, by thee unseen;
No changeless state, no permanence between;
Life's strong activities abrade the mold;
Incessant throbbing makes the heart grow old;
These co-efficients of eternal change,
If form'd to alter, must at last derange.
Thus nations rise; thus flourish, fade, decay:
The foaming mead will burst the cup of clay;
The blooming cheek can only bloom awhile;
Excess of glory lights the funeral pile.

" Beyond the frail expedient of an hour,
Beyond utility exists a Power,
Beyond the diadem's precarious light,—
The Power to see and venerate the Right.
The righteous man admiring millions call
To mold the manners and the fate of all,
Disdains to deem utility a power;
Disdains the mean expedients of the hour;
Reveres the TRUE, the GOOD, the JUST, the RIGHT,—
Eternal verities from worlds of light;
From these, from these alone, he loves to draw
His righteous edicts, fundamental law;
Keeps ever near the lamp of Time to see,
What Wisdom's path and policy may be,

A Mentor's prudence in his soul, to lay
His thread of life along the narrow way;
The eloquence of Ithaca, to show
The narrow path his people ought to go.

"I love to sit with Doctors in the law,
Propose nice questions, quaint distinctions draw,
In Forum, Court, in Legislative Hall,
To Diets, Thrones, dictate the good of all:
To talk of Justice, Freedom, Duty, Right;
I feel as in my native realms of Light.
With Solon thus I passed the midnight hour,
Taught Numa thus to hold the reins of power,
Taught Nerva, Trajan, Antonine to see,
That Truth, Right, Justice make felicity.
A mortal clothed in purple robes of state,
With Truth, Experience stationed at his gate;
Whose Conscience, quick to every generous thrill,
Sits close in cordial whispers with his Will;
Whose firm resolve is still on virtue's side,
Though Fate oppose, and factious foes deride;
To flattery deaf, undazzled by a name,
With views as large, enlightened as his aim;
Whose soul, unsoiled by low cupidity,
Adored by millions makes the millions free;
That soul becomes an Idolon divine,
The loftiest, purest in this world of thine;
Your central Sun, with radiant glory crowned,
Outweighing all the subject suns around.
One soul, endowed this moral height to soar,
Gives light and orbit to a million more.
Those sacred heights with fires of Freedom shine;
There law is love, and human life divine;

There Pandects, Codes, are but a needful chart
To mark your Edens, few and far apart.
How sweet to labor when we love the cause!
When glad obedience waits on genial laws.—
The proud barbarian boasts the name of Rome,
When cave or castle makes a genial home.
I show the world an Image, now and then,—
The bliss of man when ruled by noble men.

"Around the world, in spirit, haste to see
What men have been, and nations sought to be;
Where antique piles and moldering ruins cast
Thy heart beneath the shadows of the Past.
Wouldst taste the transport of a holy fear?
Lo! Zion, yonder! Pause a moment there.
Those glittering steeples! there a broken wall!
Mosque, minaret, arcade, monastic hall!
Come, pass the Kedron, linger by Siloam;
There gleams a bastion, here a sacred dome!
With speechless awe, by flowery Carmel stray;
Those columns wreathed with silver braid survey.
Away, by Tadmor,—o'er Persepolis:
Have mortals lived, and toiled, and strove for this!
Away, to Hellas,—round the Cyclades!
Come, muse amid the thoughts of Pericles!
Eleusis here, and there the Delphic shrine;
Grace, Beauty, Taste, Sublimity divine!
Oh! thou art shivering with emotion!—Why?—
But haste, we must not linger,—thou and I!
Baths, columns, arches,— hail! imperial Rome!
The tomb of Adrian! Lo! a Tuscan dome!
Pillars of porphyry! roofs ablaze with gold!
The Coliseum! voiceless now! Behold!

The Vatican!—Its walls alive with art!
These statues seem from marble tombs to start!
Grace, Beauty, Taste, Sublimity divine!
Hail, glorious Image!   Is it yours or mine?
The rich Agalma of some glorious thought,
From climes untrod, in glad devotion brought;
Some living Icon, bright, but undefined,
Snatched from beyond, to lure the longing Mind,
When human hands the classic bliss conveyed
To tomb and tower, to wall and colonnade.
You pass the Desert, pass the Plains, and know
That men were there in ages long ago;
And through the ashes of your buried race,
An Image of celestial life you trace;
But know,—the life of one Good Man I call
The most celestial image of them all."

A glorious world!   They say Prometheus stole
The fire of heaven to grace the human soul.
We see, Erasmus, on the shore and hill,
That heavenly essence burns with Beauty still.
Adore the blessing, and no more repine;
For man has been, and yet may be, divine.

"My golden youth might deem the world to be
Great, good, enlightened, virtuous, happy, free:
But I have seen, e'en in my budding years,
Some human misery, seen some human tears.
Man might be great and happy, if he would,
Some few enlightened, many might be good,
The bard of Mantua tells his country so,
Alas! he proves them happier than they KNOW.
We lose the image of a life divine,
We eat the dust, and grovel with the swine,

Our heart is false, our warmth, a morbid heat,
Our hate instinctive, and our love, deceit ;
We barter beauty, waste the bliss we win,
We rage or riot, roll in sloth or sin.
We fight for factions, cringe to pride and power,
And petty tyrants train us to the hour.
Art shapes the column, decorates the hall ;
Yet wields the sabre, wings the minnie ball.
Our history is a list of battle-fields ;
Our glory means the meeting of our shields.
We talk of justice, learning, liberty ;
Yet millions die that conquerors may be free.
Lords boast the work their groaning vassals did ;
Slaves rear the column, build the pyramid ;
Those marble pavements please the passing eye ;
The toil is over, and the tears are dry.
Cries, imprecations, scourges, curses sound,
Those gorgeous halls and palaces around.
Pale Memory reads on pillars high and cold,
The records red of agonies untold.
We form the Court, erect the Senate hall,
Laws, Constitutions ;—violate them all ;
Belie the Lord of Nature in his face,
And what we do not disbelieve, disgrace.
A world of truth, philosophy, and light,
With Bruno's fagot flashing on the sight !
Of Tasso's dungeon how we love to read !
We burn the martyr, then adopt the creed !
A world that boasts the Beautiful, the True,
With broken arch, and battered wall in view,
Still rolls the wheel of Juggernaut around
A world of science and of arts profound,

That boasts its tombs of marble and of sod,
And builds its temples on the grave of God!
A world that prays the Lord of love and life,
To draw his sword, and join the field of strife!
Where gelid Altai rises cold and white,
A shivering train descends the frozen height,
Through burning Cobi takes its arid way,
To fall beneath a baby's feet, and pray!
How long shall pity blush with shame to see
The rites of Boodh, the horrors of Pooree?
The abject pilgrim crawls from shore to shore
To feed the flames of Kali with his gore;
Sarmanian hordes to stormy Baikal flock,
Kneel by the wave, and venerate a rock,
While fancy sees the watery Garan sweep
From wave to wave, along the mystic deep!

"Away! away! I see no form divine.
Truth, Beauty lives, but man is not the shrine;
To mountains high, to oceans deep I go,
To brooks that murmur, to the winds that blow.
The rocks beneath, the stars that roll above,
May teach me Beauty, teach me Truth and Love;
Adieu the glory and the gates of men!
The rainbow rests upon the mountain glen."

IDOTHEA.

I.

THE BEAUTY OF TRUTH.

IDOS II.—TRUTH IN NATURE.

Ne dubita, nam Vera vides.
—VIRGIL.

BOOK II.—ANALYSIS.

Ruins.—Enquiry renewed:—First Excursus, among the tribes of flood, forest, and field;—all true to their instincts, true to their climates and seasons, their economy, their loves, their enjoyments, their destiny.

Second Excursus,—the Ancient Earth,—its recesses, History, Surfaces of Life, Mausolea;—Progression.

Third Excursus:—Planetary Systems,—true to their aspects and orbits;—Suns of first Order;—Suns of second Order;—Nebulae;—Central Sun of third Order;—Enquiries,—System,—Universe, Creation,—Sky over all.

THE BEAUTY OF TRUTH.
Idos II.

    This Summer night in starry silence brings
The far-off murmur of the mountain springs;
High rolls the moon amid her golden day,
And down our darkness bends the solar ray.
Through depths serene, a sea of silver white
Flows from the sky, and mingles with the night,
Blent, sober'd, soften'd; were the truth unknown,
I must believe this lustre all her own.
So, man, enlighten'd as he trims the vaie,
Transmits an Image, cold, indeed, and pale.
The bright conceptions, spirit-wing'd and fleet,
Approach our clay, and darken as they meet:
Our fallen powers of heart and brain impure,
Refract, distort them, intercept, obscure;
And some, whose souls the Primal Light revere,
See no reflection of the heavenly here.

    What were this world, if all that man has done
Were still renew'd, resplendent in the sun!
Each busy street, each port, and peopled mart,
Each tome of thought, each monument of art!
Ah! noon is night! Heaven opens seal by seal;
Earth heaves her bosom, and her cities reel.
Fire, inundation, tempest, lava, rain,
With mausolea strew the rolling plain;

The waste of years, the Nemesis of Time,
Dissolves the solid, levels the sublime;
The thirst of empire, odious love of war,
Allure, impel barbarians from afar;
O'er heaving pavements, rolling-eyed and tall,
The demon Discord stalks the senate hall,
The hail of Odin, winds of Ahriman,
Emerge from Gothland, darken from Touran.

    Troy, Balbec, Sidon, Memphis, Nineveh,
Have glitter'd, triumph'd, totter'd, pass'd away.
The torch of Thais fired the Magian dome,
But Thais, kneeling, fed voracious Rome:
Rome falls before the Goth, the Vandal, Hun:
Her purples clothe the race of Edecon.
Art, Genius, Empire, burning and unblest,
In fading fragments, waver down the West.
The Prophet and his Caliphs, in the East,
Devour Arabia, ravage, ruin, feast;
The Turkman, Tartar, Seljuk, Mogul sweep
O'er nations buried in inglorious sleep;
And dread Alp-Arslan, heartless Tamerlane,
Pile up with human pyramids the plain;
Art, Genius, Empire, trembled, totter'd, fell,
And floating fragments fill'd the Dardanelles.
Alas! the Moslem, pausing at Manu,
Alp-Arslan's moral may no more construe!
And here, e'en here, our native glades around,
Our swains unconscious plough the Indian Mound!
And such, alas! the dynasties of earth,
Birth feeds extinction, death evolves a birth.
The mystic curve, what calculus may find?
Ah! who may write the Iliads of mankind?

What if the rich magnificence no more,
In pristine beauty decorates the shore?
If barbarous men and unrelenting Time,
Have soil'd the lovely, level'd the sublime?
If only gleam, through shadows of the Past,
Pale fragments of the beautiful and vast?
They still are fragments of sublimity,
And gleams of heaven, and lofty mind you see,
If wrapp'd in ruins, on the vale or hill,
We find a jewel, 'tis a jewel still ;
The spark hath come through some immortal soul,
Though Ruin swell around it to the pole.
Whence came the thought, so beautiful, so pure?
And whence the art that makes that thought endure?
And where the Source, the Fountain, the Supreme?
This sparkling gem is but the last extreme.

Does Nature shed from starry vault, or flower,
This bright conception, this immortal power?
In bird, or beast, or mountain, shall we find,
The source of thought, the antetype of mind?
Oh! there is Beauty in the blooming flower,
The mountain minstrel, and the vocal bower,
The sea, the stream, the sunbeam, and the star,
The cloud careering on its golden car ;
The lambent lightning, and the mystic play
Of gliding meteor down the Milky Way !
Earth, heaven, is grace, sublimity around ;
The roar of Ocean, in his caves profound ;
The loud volcano thundering at the sky ;
Yon azure tent, so limitless and high ;
The thunder rolling on the clouded height,
The rush of storm, and majesty of night,

From these, perchance, the musing soul may draw
Thought, Genius, Impulse, Inspiration, Law;
And these, perchance, may be the first extreme.—
The Centre, Source, the Primitive, Supreme.
No fresher did this bright Agalma shine,
When Homer, Phidias felt the thrill divine.
Ah! over all a living Love must rise,
And meet the Spirit in the earth and skies.
And if amid the ruins of mankind,
Be lost the Light that thrill'd the ancient mind.
From star and sky, this silent Summer night,
Comes not the glory of that ancient Light?
Hail, Light divine! Adieu, the barren shore!
A nearer, holier vision, if no more!

"Trust no illusion! Stricken and subdued,
To thee I fly from thought and solitude;
I seek again the friendly gates of men,—
The rainbow rests upon a monster's den.
I sought to find one summer day's retreat
From toil, and strife, and traffic, and deceit,
From rant of rapture, thoughtlessness of thought,
From fears of fog, and hopes that end in naught.
Vile mockeries of mercy, justice, truth,
The games of age, the frolic crimes of youth,
From altar, victim, sacrifice, and shrine,
And all the trumpery we CALL divine.
An hour among the meads and lanes I stray'd;
A rill comes winding down a mountain glade,
Its banks all fragrant with the bloom of June,
Its waters sparkling underneath the moon.
An open pasture, redolent and wide;
A woody slope ascending at each side;

The grassy level, narrowing on the view,
Winds in the Massanutten like a screw.
There flocks lay slumbering on the grassy vale;
And herds, hoarse-breathing in the lustre pale,
With dusky bulks, half seen between the trees,
Lay on the slopes, reclined on bended knees.
I clomb among them from the pastoral lawn,
And met the sweet serenity of dawn.
A freshness, soothing to the brow, was there,
And yet no sound, no movement of the air.

"The fading stars reluctantly withdrew
Their keen regard, and dark the coppice grew;
A fleecy paleness overspread the moon,
And orient airs began their whispers soon,
And far the tall oracular pines above,
Passed something like the first faint smile of love:
And something seem'd to whisper down from heaven,
'Awake, my sweetest minstrel of the seven!
Ye happy tenants of the wood and lawn,
Arise, my loves, and drink the joys of dawn!'
Long, misty lines, of dim, uncertain hue
Reach'd forth, divergent, underneath the blue,
Suffused the stars, and, sloping down the West,
Set rose and ruby in the lunar crest.
Earth lean'd to meet the coming Deity,
And mountains hurried from the West to see.
The orient lines are misty now no more;
The golden reins are flashing at the door;
The gate unfolds,—Time's ancient songs begin;
The king of glory and of day comes in!
Hail, Beauty, Light, Sublimity divine!
This, this is Morning! Guido, what is thine?

"A mossy seat beneath an oak I found:
The golden sunbeams waver'd, danced around;
For amorous airs were whispering in the trees,
And shadows pass'd of motes, and birds, and bees.
I sat and view'd the playful lawn below,
The slope beyond, all radiant in the glow:
The skipping lamb that knew the name of "Ma,"
The young ewe, nodding with responsive BAA;
The calves and cattle, winding down the hill,
The bounding roe that came to sip the rill;
While wide above the thrush, the linnet, jay,
In choral joy, attun'd their morning lay:
The woodland Orpheus, learned in the score
Of mountain minim and mimetic lore;
The royal eagle, mounting to the sky,
With poising pinion, and undazzled eye.
The social crow convened from rock and lea
His black convention on the old dry tree;
There built the State, reformed, repealed the law,
Their longest speech the archetypal CAW.
The glancing robin, with his breast of red,
Kept flitting near to treasure what was said;
The pheasant, with hereditary drum,
Drumm'd the old log, and told the rain to come,
While turtles coo'd, in cooler shades alone,
Their bars of mellow, melancholy tone:
The bee, the fly, untaught their joys to sing,
Buzz'd out the bliss, with green and golden wing,
And insects, creeping from their holes of clay,
Crawled in the sheen, and drank the balm of day."

And here, I say, the laws of Nature reign,
Pure, unaffected, genial, simple, plain;

The conscious heart of some untainted race,
Pulsates with joy each living inch of space.
E'en marsh malaria, oozing in the heat,
Regales a sense that finds malaria sweet.
There Nature, true to season, tide, and time,
Fills, feeds, adapts, adorns the teeming clime.
Abyss of Wonder! mystery divine!
Blind, mindless Nature, can the work be thine?
See order, system, rank, gradation, plan,
From moss to oak, from polypus to man;
A vast, complex economy of joy,
Transmitting life as still the years destroy.

Love, Beauty, Rapture!—Which is most divine?
Who mix'd a joy in all the beams that shine?
Airs might have breath'd, the sun, the star have shone,
Still bliss, love, beauty, been to earth unknown.
Birds might have built the nest, purvey'd the meal,
Unfelt the joys that tender parents feel;
Yet something plann'd the transports of a heart,
With kindest, sweetest, most endearing art;
And something brings these Æons from the sky,
To live in dust, and leave that dust to die.
I see not how the lifeless mote could know
The force, or weight of luxury or woe;
How rock, or tree, or fountain gets the mind
To feel a pain, or hasten to be kind;
How Kindness, Pain, Delight, Affection start
In circling atoms, beating with a heart.
Ah! no!—the Pain, the Love, the Transport spring
Beyond the sphere of each material thing,—
A boon of heaven, an Image all divine,
Inwrought, inwoven with the beams that shine;

The sparkling drops of supersensual dew,
Born in the depths of unapparent blue,
That kiss the dust, and, kissing, still exalt;
Then bound, undying, to their native vault.

"The ancient customs still direct the grove:
There rival fashions, flirting never strove.
Cosmetics, cushions, flounces, frills unknown.
They live content with Nature's charms alone;
Secure to please, no artful guise they seek,
No paints or patches for a faded cheek;
No polish'd plate of steel, or brass, to show
The tinge of rouge, or fit of furbelow.
Or, if a stream their graceful forms display,
None, like Narcissus, gaze and pine away.
Unsandal'd still they roam the hill, the moor,
Nor purchase slaves to lay a marble floor.
Their carpets green the airs of heaven perfume.
They need no labors of Edonian loom.
There all unknown duplicity of soul,
The secret poniard, or the poisoned bowl,
These build no bonfires, light no banquet hall,
Nor, red with slaughter, raise a Fancy Ball.
No gambler here infests the heath or hill.
No fiery fluid issues from the still.
No prisons here, no pyramids, no towers,
Their home the hills, their citadel the bowers.
Unstudied here the waltz and serenade.
Not e'en a fox conceives a masquerade.
Armorial ensigns, shields, no less obscure,
Though long their lineage, and that lineage pure.
Star, garter, ribbon, coronation, cross,
Uncurrent here for grass, or fragrant moss.

No cells monastic, convents, shrines have they,
No beads to reckon, and no tithes to pay.
No day condemn'd to penance, prayer, or fast;
They range the plains, and find a free repast.
Their faith is one, no heretics you see,
No rite or ritual, pope or papacy,
Yet heaven's regard and Nature's wealth they share,
Nor saint, nor sage, can find an atheist there.

"No: true, obedient to a pulse within,
They live, rejoice, nor deem that joy a sin;
They live, they love, and feel that love secure,
A law of Nature, and like Nature, pure;
A grace consigned like azure to the sky,
Warmth to the ray, or vision to the eye.

"Rapt with the Muse, I lost the sense of sound,
And tuneful songs were heard no more around.
"And what," I asked, "are happiness and love?
Are they of dust, or come they from above?
A breeze, a breath from summit, plain, abyss,
Warm Inspirations from yon worlds to this?
The waves of life all sparkle as they flow,
And every sparkle is a joy below.
For something warm, benevolent, and sweet,
Weds Life and Light in rapture, when they meet.
This nameless something, is it not divine,
The touch of God, the glory of Design?
Truth, Reason, Wisdom, supercosmal cause,
Commission'd, moved in these material laws.
And something more than Intellect can show:
The smiles of Goodness permeate below,
And make the chords of sentient Life respond
To high, mysterious harmonies beyond.

Fair is the blade that waves upon the green,
And fair the leaf that shades the sylvan scene,
The drop that falls, the limpid rill that flows,
The flower that blooms, the whispering air that blows,
Sounds sweetly murmur in the genial breeze,
Sweet buds adorn, sweet fruits enrich the trees,
And sweet, ethereal is the shining ray,
That comes at morn, and gives the golden day.
Oh! bliss to bound in freedom o'er the plain!
When day is done, to rest—to sleep again;
With Love on earth and Guardians in the sky,
To live is bliss; it may be bliss to die!
Carol, ye birds; ye lambs, exult below!
Lo! ye are happy, happier than ye know;
Go, friendly bee, go, sip the balmy dews,
And leave me here to banquet with the Muse.

"If Beauty be the vesture of the True,
Life, Love, Enjoyment, Goodness, what are you?
Are those the old divinities I see?
The Dryad maidens peeping from the tree?
Indeed, it seems the gnomes and Naiads fair,
The Nereids, Nymphs sport in the wave, the air;
And Nornas hasten from the sacred well,
With urns divine from Hela, where they dwell,
And bathe the roots of Igdrasil below,
Till mountains sing, and dust begins to grow.
Ho! every mote that wanderest in the ray,
Come to the waters;—Nature feasts to-day!
Clothe thee in flesh, rejoice, and sing, and shine,
For life is bliss, and Beauty is divine!
What millions crowd the little space I see!
The blade, the leaf, the rill, the rock, the tree!

All glad and grateful for the boundless store;
The cups are filled they just have drain'd before.
They drink the fountains, still the fountains flow,
They seize the berries, and new berries grow!
Grass turns to flesh, to life the limpid wave;
These feast in turn, and taste the bliss they gave!"

I learn each form of insect, bird, or beast,
Which now exults, and shares the common feast,
Is woven all of atomies unseen,
Won from the airs, the waters, and the green.
I ask this grain that glitters in my hand,
"Canst thou behold me, canst thou understand?
Canst thou rejoice, or taste the sweets of love,
Or learn the melody of lark or dove!
O, bright Accession! drop, or breath, or ray,
Infuse, inform this voiceless grain with day!
Come, now, commission'd from the courts above,
And fill this grain, with song, and joy, and love!"
Ah, me! They wait a mightier voice than mine;
They hide, they mock me,—deep in the Divine;
I fashion, mold this atom as I may;
I call for Joy, but Joy will not obey."

"Warm'd with the gladness of each living thing,
Voluptuous Fancy spread her purple wing.
I pass'd the lakes, the rivers, and the seas;
I heard new songs of rapture in the breeze;
Drawn from the depths of bright and breaking waves,
I drank the murmurs of the emerald caves;
All motion, rapture, animation, love,
The Joy below leap'd to the Joy above;
O'er silent Siwah, and the gardens fair
Of Irem, groves of Indian spices rare.

I breathed awhile Arabian airs of balm,
Pass'd Arctic, Tropic, and the Groves of Palm,
Where olives, citrons, figs, bananas grow,
Where life and love in warmer currents flow.

"O, heaven!" I cried, "is this a world of sin?
With blessings rare, and raptures hard to win?
Zones, islands, oceans, continents of feast,
With bleeding victim, deprecating priest?
Milk, Nectar, Eden, for the lips, the eyes,
With altars fuming to avenging skies?
Bright seas! green islands! Where does woe begin?
Where terrors, tortures, wrath, destruction, sin?
Are these, too, Symbols of that nameless Power,
Who sends the sunbeam and the genial shower?
And still the new interrogation woke
From sea and summit, mountain pine and oak;
And golden hours in dreamy lapse withdrew,
I look'd! The heavens were robed in sable hue;
My dream was o'er. The winds were all unbound:
The lightnings quiver'd in the glens profound.
Mysterious change! The summits waved and bow'd,
The growling thunder mutter'd in the cloud.
The forest roar'd, the herds had all withdrawn,
And darkness lay recumbent in the lawn.
I shelter'd, where the herdsmen sheltered oft, –
A covert rude, —and scann'd the clouds aloft.
An angry blackness; up the sky they came,
Each moment seamed with heaven-avenging flame.
The vengeance came. Down to the root was cleft,
By one red bolt, the oak I just had left;
And hurl'd, unbreathing, at my covert door,
Fell the poor dove that coo'd an hour before!

What had she done?   Alas!   What could she do?
Why had she lived, or why been taught to coo?
The rain was down.   The tempest broke away,
And struggling through, shone-out the closing day.
The morning rill, an evening torrent grown,
Tumbled and foamed to drown a mother's moan:
The heartless waters, pitiless of pain,
Had seized a lamb, and swept it from the plain.
In tears and horror, through the dusk I flew,
Glad to regain my native vale, and you."

   The flood, the bolt have brought two atoms more,
To integrate the charnel vaults of yore:
Two deaths, to make the miles of death eleven,
From crystal granite to the crystal heaven.
For this, the torrent sweeps the lamb away:
For this, the lightning leaps the hills, to slay:
Mild ministers of Nature's wise behest,
They stop the breath, they put the heart to rest:
They fossilize our planetary crust:
Restore to dust the revenue of dust.
A thousand Æons have they marr'd and made,
Built tribes of clay, and tribes in ruin laid:
Wind, water, fire, their willing tribute pay,
Prepared to bless, nor less prepared to slay.
Life, death distribute down the hills afar,
And change eternal speeds his bickering car.
Ah! dreams are memories,—fragments of the True:
The Titans rear their Babel's to the blue;
And Yotuns streamed from Yotunheim indeed,
When milodons went crashing through the reed!
Ah! thunders in the nether halls of fire,
Have echoed long, have muttered hoarse and dire:

And hail, and flame, and avalanche have done
Bold deeds of death beneath the gazing sun :
Siroccos swept the continents of green,
And earthquakes heaved in hills the level scene.
Thou didst not hear the thunders of the deep,
When Old Creations stagger'd into sleep :
Thou hast not traced the torrent fierce and red,
By flaming homes and hamlets of the dead,
When hundred-handed Briareus again,
Unbar'd the rocks, and heaved the boiling main :
When waters redden'd in the molten deep,
And trees, unsmoking, vanish'd from the steep,
And fiery oceans, roll'd upon the shore,
Submerge, restore a continent,—no more !
The Andes tower, the Alleghanies spread
Their social summits, flaming still and red ;
The gleaming porphyry, cooling on the height,
Sheds o'er the vales a melancholy light ;
The vales are filled with monsters of the deep,
Boiled, mangled, piled, in everlasting sleep !

When columns, gleaming like a Gothic spire,
Assailed the clouds, with hungry tongues of fire,
And busy lightnings gleam'd in laughter round,
With thunders pealing under, o'er the ground :
Then came afar, from out the lurid blue,
The breathing Infinite, with cooling dew,
Moved o'er the deep, repressed the surging flame.
Barr'd the mad tumult down in granite frame :
On high, obedient thunders pealing loud,
To streaming torrents melt the yielding cloud.
The yellow floods descend the rocky steep,
And Nereus built his palace in the deep.

The power infused, new laws of ORDER reign,—
The fair cosmothesis of grain with grain.
The solid rocks obey the voice of Fate;
Attract, repel, combine, disintegrate;
The crystal spreads in beds of dolomite,
The coral climbs, and coils the ammonite;
Opposing powers, commingled fire and snow;
Swift Ariels here, grim Nephalim below;
O'er breezy dales, subsiding from the strife,
The breathing Ruah drops the seeds of life:
Then first the fern, the moss, the calamite,
Wave on the rock, and woo the genial light;
Then first the green, outspread beneath the blue,
From sun and shower its stores of progress drew;
The plant and molusk, first declining, gave
A holy grace—the memories of a grave;
Then Death evoked from shell, and fern, and reed,
Rich fields of growth, and mines for human need.

"Descend the Trappa of this fossil quire,
Clay, slate, coal, marble, porphyry, granite, fire;
From rock to flesh, from vertebra to mind,
Retrace the ages, dim and undefined;
Review the races which from stone began,
Shell, Saurian, Coral, Bird, Leviathan;
Death locks them all with shaly bar and line,
In beds bituminous, and Parian mine;
Death, faithful Treasurer of Life and Fate,
Imbeds, embalms whate'er the Powers create.
Life does the work which naught but Life can do,
Death strews the bed which Death alone can strew,—
The vital plain, whence nobler forms shall spring,
Till Death, advancing, round a nobler ring,

H

And rising powers of intellect shall date
Still brighter rings of life, and death, and fate.

"Ah, me! we find no Terra Firma here!
Our hull of rock is not for us to steer;
Our keel of granite swims on seas of flame,
And nether thunders rock its stony frame;
And breathing instinct long has learned to know
The throbbings of its fiery heart below.
Our decks, forever scooped by flood and rain,
Ere long shall bowl the restless seas again;
These vales embower the creatures of the deep,
And watery monsters scale the watery steep.
Thus, ever thus, our waving film vibrates,
Sinks, swells, declines beneath the molding Fates,
While star and sun, with unremitting ray,
See greener fields still rising to the day,
And glad Improvement steps from sea to shore,
And hermit Hope sits waiting still for more.

"Ah! drear the day, and drear the starless night,
Ere granite lobes enshrined the trilobite;
Ere earth and heaven were linked in mutual love,
The finite here, the infinite above;
Distinct, yet blended, wedded, yet unbound,
Revealed in life, and blooming from the ground:
That ever fleeting, growing but ungrown;
This, changeless, radiant, limitless, unknown;
That, ever rounding into forms that live,
This, hovering, whispering, life and love to give;
That, bound in worlds, in elements combined,
This, felt in Truth, and worshiped in the mind;
That, of progression, order, rank, the source,
This, of sensation, motion, feeling, force.

"Is it an evil to be called away
From huts of mud and tenements of clay,
(E'en if we leave our rotten rags behind,)
To lighted halls and banquets of the mind?
The conscious life which fill'd the hapless lamb,
Shall fill again the virgin clay with balm,
In fairer form shall walk the flowery plain,
Endued with joys that triumph over pain.
That spark of life, escaped the smitten dove,
Shall light a brow with lineaments of love,
And syllable along the vocal tongue,
Bright thoughts that never had been felt or sung.
The form we love, and dress with gaudy care,
And wipe our mirrors, to behold how fair,
Turn'd, view'd, admir'd, with all the zest of pride,
Is ripe for Nature when it shall have died.

"From darkness, dust, the germ begins to grow,
Warm'd from above, and suckled from below;
The genial powers of sun, and rain, and air,
To foster, feed, from cloud and sky repair.
The living thing, in green, expanding pride,
Inhales the breeze, inhales the golden tide.
In radiant tiers its branching arms extend,
Reach out for life, with graceful curve and bend;
A thousand leaves with spiracles besprent,
Breathe, waver, feed, beneath the azure tent.
The luscious treasures of each year secured,
Enwrap the bole, in snowy vest matured;
And ages come, and human ages go,
The oak endures, the bole and branches grow.
Then comes, at last, up from the nether sea,
That voice which chill'd the young Antigone:

"Ho! Œdipus, why linger we to go?
Thou, thou hast long been wanted here below."
And hungry Death with grim, obedient toil,
Secures the wealth, and lays the dark brown soil.

In darkness, too, the embryon life unfolds,
When plastic law his third creation molds.
Wrought, knit, inwoven, vein, and nerve, and bone,
With eyes to see, and feet to move alone;
Green earth receives it, and it treads the plain;
It feels a current warm in every vein.
A throbbing heart is beating at its side;
It looks, and lo! a world of verdure wide.
In crowds of kindred, visitors around,
It leaps, it runs, it gambols o'er the ground.
In balmy sleep its night revolves away,
In feast and fun, its warm, voluptuous day.
Strange Alchemist!—a miracle divine,
Flowers change to flesh, as water changed to wine,
A giant mass of muscle, nerve, and bone,
Stalks the savannas, built of grass alone.
Wild, strange emotions thrill the moving frame,
Sweet loves attract, and jealousies inflame;
Till old and huge, in flesh and frame mature,
It carries all that Nature would secure;
And Nature's voice, the sacred voice of Death,
Arrests the mass, and draws the giant's breath;—
"Thou too hast long been wanted here below;
Ho! Œdipus, why linger we to go?"

Thus Life and Death, divine, congenial powers,
Improve, adorn this rolling world of ours,
They serve, they work with consentaneous toil,
Enrich the quarry, fertilize the soil.

But man, a wanderer, steps upon the scene;
He finds, he feels himself a link between,
A link between the fossil links below,
And golden links, he hopes some day to know;
A restless searcher, toss'd from hope to fear,
If destined yonder, or if bounded here.
He cannot see that gifts of heart and head,
Would form a strata, when his race is dead;
That Faith and Hope, pure Reason, Thought divine,
Would crystallize, and build some Parian mine.
The frame he feeds of vein, and nerve, and bone,
By Death secured, may crystallize to stone,
He cannot see what Nature meant to do
With lofty Thought, Conceptions of the True;
With blissful visions and immortal song,
With tomes of logic, codes of right and wrong;
Elysian fancies, and the happy Isles,
Where Virtue dwells, celestial Wisdom smiles;
With treasured systems of the True, the Fair,
With Reason throned amid the treasures there,
With all the stores his brain can make or find,
The rich Principia of laborious Mind;
Stores, gather'd not from rain, or rock, or light,
Of heavenly source, of empyrean height;
With all that tongue can mold in mortal breath,
Can these be wanted for the vaults of Death?

And yet he sees Creation's onward aim,
For all that live, for all that Death may claim;
Till old and musing, half afraid to go,
He hears a whisper stealing down below,
He hears a far-off whisper in the sky:
"Ho! Œdipus, why linger we to fly?"

"Thy words are healing, balmy as the breeze,
When Summer evening hives the wand'ring bees.
I should be silent, grateful, satisfied,
Though gentle ones, and beautiful have died.
We half believe that which we MUST believe;
I only grieve to see much cause to grieve.
I own the high benevolence, to give
A shrub, a shell, prerogative to live.
I grant it better as a shell to die,
Than ever senseless as a rock to lie;
To flower the mead, to greet the hills awhile,
Than lost forever in some granite pile.

"I, too, can read a Goodness, Power divine,
In faded flower, in stony coralline;
Bright images of Deity I see
In beds of stone, in dust of fallen tree.
Oh! deeper, colder, drearier far the gloom,
To see a lifeless world without a tomb!
We live among the sepulchres of old;
To me the grave endears the rocky wold.
The dust of Adam at my feet is spread;
The air is sweet with memories of the dead,
And sweeter, lovelier is the world to me,
For all the dear memorials I see.
But I would love a Deity all love,
All light, benevolence, below, above;
A God of power and prescience to express
His love in worlds of lasting happiness;
I love the bright progression, which hath run
From mite to milodon, from mote to sun;
I greet Improvement, rising up in air,
From rock to reed, from mine to city fair.

But why Progression, why Improvement grow
From nerves of pain, and tenements of woe?
Here thrills a discord, grates a jarring sound,
With all the heavenly harmonies around.

"How glad I feel, at Summer eve to choose
Some moonlit summit, spirit-tuned, to muse,
With pencil, paper, mold my formulæ
Of sign and symbol, by the silver ray,
Mass, motion, centre, limit, fluxion, rate,
Of fluent orbit and co-ordinate!
This spot I take my zero-point to be
Of radius, angle, weight, velocity,
Curve, axis, function, increment, I bind
In pregnant hieroglyphics of the mind.
Lo! plastic reciprocities dilate ; .
The yielding forms beneath my hand equate;
The generous powers, obedient as I mold,
Expand, develop, integrate, unfold.
I see fair images, unseen before,
Lurk, hiding, smiling, in my woven lore:
Young, rosy cherubs,—truths and laws of art,—
Like playful Dryads, from the forest start;
Long-hidden springs, and principles divine,
From Nature's bosom, rise in term and sign;
The social ties of comet, planet, sun,—
The Olams run, the harmonies to run.
All Nature's genial, bright Economy,
Unveiling here, in anaglyphs I see.
No piers sustain, no granite walls secure,
Yet systems roll, and central suns endure.
I touch with awe this slowly throbbing heart;
The pulses come, and tranquilly depart ; ·

Each vital heave scarce stirs the lightest dew,
Yet distant worlds are speeding up the blue ;
The largest profit with the smallest cost ;
No vain exaction, no exertion lost.
One centre keeps its unimpeded course,
With conservation of the living force,
And willing, glad velocities afar,
Absorb the weight of planet, system, star!"

Thy plan, my son, is Nature's modest plan ;
Truth comes alone in Images to man ;
Too bright and bashful for the mortal eye,
She drops her shadow, as she hurries by.
No mortal sees a ray of light direct ;
We see alone what cloud and sky reflect.
And if from rule or formula of thine,
Thou hast evoked one Image thus divine,
Look up, behold a formula on high,
Not idly drawn to decorate the sky ;
Look up, and, reading, learn a deeper lore ;
Truth loves to smile on whom she smiled before.

"I love to look ; far more to speed away,
Not uninvited, yet with some dismay;
A youthful stranger, too untaught to roam,
Should find his fitting pupilage at home.
But feeling I can make myself to be
Uncoiled by flesh, unchained by gravity ;
While resting here my passive limbs remain,
I step from earth, and tread the solar plain,
A wider stratum, more resplendent field,
Than all your beds of shifting ocean yield.

"O, bliss ! unbound by breathing dust, to skim,
Free, swift as thought, these paths and spaces dim !

To meet the winged spirits of the sky,
In level phalanx, as they wander by;
Meet light out-flowing on the worlds, in gold,
Life, throbbing, thrilling, as the clouds unfold,
Mysterious powers, that clothe the world in green
Stream from the sun, and hasten by unseen.
His radiant arms o'er subject worlds extend,
Reach, touch their orbits, and the orbits bend.
Each comet brings from systems, suns, afar,
Legations high, on perihelion car.
Thrones, powers, dominions crowd his flaming courts,
Reveal their missions, lay their sage reports,
Secure, extend the sacred ties of old,
With shining cords, and brighter chains of gold.
O'er all the plain, sage Senators appear,
From orb, and ring, and silver moon, and sphere.
Afar from hall and planetary dome,
Swift cars traverse the blazing hippodrome.
Interpreter and wanded vestiare,
In royal state, around the king repair.
Ah! swarming Themes, in robes of radiant white,
Throng, cluster, crowd the echoing halls of light.
I hoped to reach his Audience Room alone,
And lay my one dark question at his throne:
"Oh! tell me why, celestial Lord of life,
Thy blessings all are mix'd with toil and strife?
O, Sun! what Image of the Good is there,
In limbs that bleed, and burning hearts that sear?"

" Nor may I find a full solution here;
For other realms, and brighter suns appear;
A thousand centres, beaming light and life
To subject worlds, no doubt of toil and strife,

A thousand galleries of transcendent art,
Foil'd by the anguish of some bursting heart;
Sublime displays of Goodness, Wisdom, Power,
To multiply the parting, dying hour!
Oh! fly I must! On wings of wonder fly
To every sun that blazes in the sky;
From plain to plain, from zone to azure zone,
In wild amazement, plead at every throne:
"Is there no holy Narthex in the throng
Of rolling Fires, these azure plains along,
No sacred Vestry, no Triclinium far
In deep abysses of some triple star,
Where triple orbs reciprocal diffuse
On blooming worlds their complemental hues?
Why rear this august city in the sky,
For hearts to sunder, and for loves to die?
Why swell with Hope a shivering soul to see
This blazing segment of Infinity,
Broad, rounded strata, plain o'er shining plain,
Of sun, and moon, and land, and rolling main,
Of zone and tropic, pole and Milky-Way,
The Base, the Crown, that make a Nebula,
If woo'd to gaze, and warm'd with life to love
The fair, the fond, that bloom below, above,
That bursting soul, when hopes begin to bloom,
Must lay its Bliss and Beauty in the tomb!"

"The suns are silent,—heartlessly they shine;
They hear no question, heed no plea of mine!
Oh! cruel suns! be not so proud of light!
Ye have no shadows, but ye make the night.
In what sweet region is my lost Elaine?
No word,—no whisper! Need I ask again?

"No horoscope or deferent I try,
Aspect, nor dim nativity on high,
Nor gauge your trine ascendencies, to know
The fate of nations, fate of kings below.
I may be dazzled with excess of light;
But systems still are rolling on the sight;
A gleaming universe of countless suns,
Its day of days, its age of ages runs.
Where is the bright, the strong Hyperion, where?
That shapes its seasons, rules its mighty year?
I must away, where system, sun shall be
One twinkling point of purity to me.
On wings of thought, from steep to steep I soar:
Sun, system shows a parallax no more;
Adieu the stars, the firmanent I knew,
Where broad Orion fixed the wandering view.

"I pierce, unblamed, the last Ecliptic plain;
I feel, I breathe the Central air again.
Bright ministers on flashing wings I see,
Descend in millions from the Galaxy.
A double Sun, of white and ruby flame,
Warms, wields, illumines this tremendous frame;
Twin orbs of light, controlling and controlled,
With arms fraternal round each other rolled;
Each circled wide with worlds of every hue,
Green, waving woodlands, oceans broad and blue,
Sweet valleys bathed in erubescent ray,
And mountains mantled with eternal day.
Boast not, O Sun! to whom my birth behove
Your rings of Saturn, and your moons of Jove;
I knew THESE Worlds would deign to make reply;
Pride dwells below, humility on high.

These, 'blest with orbits nearer the Divine,
Their golden paths and epicycles twine;
These, unimplored, from wave and woodland show
The bliss they cherish, and the truths they know.
I would not press the dark inquiry here,
Of limbs that bleed, and burning hearts that sear,
It must be joy, o'er beauties such to sigh;
It must be bliss, in such a world to die!

"In silent wonder, let me pause to scan
The boundless splendors of this glorious plan;
This dual centre of a dual frame,
This Delphic shrine with some immortal name,
Groups, clusters, systems, fields of light serene,
With blue and fearful distances between.
Could souls that lisp their syllables in sound,
Define the lofty, fathom the profound,
And wrap the vast Conception in a word,
To earth unknown, by human ears unheard,
That Word would make its orbit in the mind,
And shine forever to redeem mankind.
Ah! here are tongues, with joyful trust I feel;
New modes of speech which may that word reveal;
Melodious tongues, beyond the pall and bier,
Which pious ears and humble hearts may hear:
And trusting still, content in feeble lay,
I gaze, conceive, and name it Nebula;
I sound the depth,— the length, the height explore,
And find there must be still one centre more.
This double Sun hath found an orbit too;
It rolls, revolves with all its retinue.
Construction in construction, wide and vast;
One centre more Creation makes, the last.

Some Mind Supreme hath fixed the high decree,
The mystic, strong necessities of THREE!
Shall I desist, retrace my daring way,
Back to the shadows and the dreams of clay?
Shall I presume, on reverent wing to try
Those primal, deep recesses of the sky,
Where all these systems, galaxies shall be
One dim and distant Nebula to me?

"O, vain to linger! Lo! I worship there!
I hear no sound; I breathe no vital air;
I feel a warmth, but not the warmth I felt
When weary oft by Lynville stream I knelt.
Visions of dreamy prophecy and song,
And Love, and Truth, and Virtue's sainted throng,
And Peace, and Liberty, and sacred Home,
Where souls redeem'd forever cease to roam;
Of distant exile, memories sad and sweet,
Of Life, and Death, and loves that longed to meet,
Of parting hours, and verdant graves afar,
In many a world, bedew'd by many a star,
Dear visions all, they come as I behold
This primitive CREATION, wall'd with gold;
And look away, and see above, below,
Resplendent Beings come, and pass, and go.
Far to that distant Nebula of ours,
The new dominion of more recent powers.
And lo! four thousand Nebulæ I see,
Dim on the bosom of Immensity;
New firmaments with countless suns bestrown,
The Stereoma of the Eldest Throne.
I feel a voice pervade me through and through!
"Be faithful ever! All is right—All True!

Life, never-dying, toil, and death, and change
Transmit the soul, and elevate its range."

   The Lord of Nature loves the number three;
The symbol of his own Immensity.
No air-drawn Image, fanciful and fond;
Man's true ideal—none may reach beyond;
State, kingdom, empire, puissant or small;
And Nature makes the last encompass all,
Rill, river, ocean, feeding and re-fed;
Untwist the light—the yellow, blue, and red.
Creation, cluster, system—wheel in wheel,
Inwoven with an everlasting Seal;
But take the wise, the living head away,
State, Kingdom, Empire—what abstractions they?
What blind, mechanic power, in space inane,
Could poise creation's adamantine chain?
The Great Sebastos sits serene above,
Molds, moves, illumines, animates with love,
Directs, restrains, with unopposed command,
Rolls clusters round, and holds them in his hand.

   " And hence a truth we tyros learn to trace,
"Three lines the least that may inclose a space."
Lo, system, cluster, Universe we see
Created, bound to Orders, Centres three.
To each he gave, in Time's primeval hour,
Its own paternal, yet dependent power.
Throne, Power, Dominion,—sun controlling sun,—
He called; they rose. He spake, and it was done.
His first Idolion—Eldest Born of light,
Emerged, and stood rejoicing in his sight;
With weight, and warmth, and majesty endued,
To rule the teeming, wild Infinitude.

From age to age, replenish'd, reimproved;
All winding, moving,—yet itself unmoved.
Thence dual Orbs, in radiant lines appear,
With clustering clouds of rolling system, sphere;
Each sphere a sun, amid a choral shower;
The Third in glory, as the last in power;
With new creations, rising, rolling far,
In system, cluster, dual Orb, and Star,
And bound and basking in the blended ray,
Of solar, medial, empyreal day;
With inward laws, expanding year by year,
To clothe, improve, remodel every sphere,
That man may see, and wondering seraphs know,
Whatever grows, has once begun to grow;
That mind may soar, and soaring, learn to find
The hidden Light of uncreated Mind.

"Oft have I seen the Summer cloud distil
Its radiant treasure on the woody hill;
The golden drops divide the evening beam,
And build an arch of Beauty o'er the stream.
And strange, I thought, that things unseen and small,
Could form an arch, by harmony of all!
Lo! here I see the radiant worlds descend,
In paths of light, that interweave and blend,
That wreathe, and curve, and harmonize, and twine
Around the throne of Truth and Love divine.
There is a sky, expanding over all,
Sun, system, sign—the measureless, the small;
Creation lifts her stereoma there,
A blue and beauteous tent for every sphere;
And harmless lightning plays along the plains,
With golden clouds and unavenging rains;

And sun, and star, and worlds of every hue,
To people space, are dropping from the Blue,
And still the Infinite, as ages loom,
Smiles in the boundless charity of room.

IDOTHEA.

I.

BEAUTY OF TRUTH.

IDOS III.—TRUTH IN REVELATION.

Δοιητέ μοι καλῶ γενέσθαι τἀνδοθεν.
                                        PLATO.

Thou desirest Truth in the Inward Parts.
                                        KING DAVID.

BOOK III.—ANALYSIS.

Cheerfulness,—Sense.—Intuition—.The Sensualist,—The Mystic,—The Skeptic,—Pagan World,—Temples and Oracles,—Oracles of Truth,—Prophets,—Beauty of their Revelations,—Pure Spirit,—Idea of Power, Wisdom, Goodness:—Attributes of Truth,—The Word;—Incarnation of Truth. Humanity exalted. Immortality,—Empire of Truth,—Voice of Wisdom.

BEAUTY OF TRUTH.

Idos III.

When social embers tramp the coming snow,
And languid Time sits dozing in the glow;
When silent maidens, ranged the hearth around,
Gaze on the coals, and know the boding sound;
When broken pauses lull the distant mill,
And howling Winter roars upon the hill,
The pulse of Nature, lingering at the heart,
To check and eye a sober gloom impart.
But why, Erasmus, why that pallid brow,
When generous Nature breathes and smiles as now?
Lo! sadness wraps thee, like a garment round,
While flowers and fruits are laughing from the ground.
The meads are dreaming of the coming day:
How sweet they rest, and wait the morning ray!
For fresher gales, and brighter blooms, they know,
Will spring the hills, and spread the vales below.
Soft underneath the hushed, incumbent air,
They press the moonbeams to their bosoms fair,
And drink the light of starry skies above,
In Nature's ecstacy, and Nature's love.
Oh! share the bliss! The bounty all is thine;
The day is human, but the night divine;
Or say why Goodness, more than man can weigh,
Can make thy brow no grateful thought betray?

"Ah! me! though finding what I seek to find,
My heart recedes; old shadows claim the mind.
Last night, you know, my hopes were led again,
From sun to sun, from plain to starry plain;
Amid the flaming vortices I saw
The Ancient Shrine of universal law;
Presumed to stand by Nature's Eldest Fire,
Saw worlds advance, revolving suns retire;
And through that First of shining magnitudes,
Where storm, nor flood, nor avalanche intrudes;
Where land and sky, and living thing, and sea,
Lie unconvulsed in rich maturity:
Transmitted there one most benignant Face,
Shone smiling from the blue, ethereal space.
Of that dear Face, in childhood's golden hour,
Oft had my heart relenting felt the power.
I may not tell the beaming love and grace
Forever bright on that maternal Face.

"But here, alas! I find my heart again;
The vision gone—that smile I seek in vain:
And with it faded, mid the stars away,
The world, the vision brighter than the day.
And naught is here but unsubstantial show,
A dreamy, cheating, everlasting flow
Of falling, fading, fleeting sound and hue,
Cold link by link still gliding from the view.
I find no living joy, to heed or hear,
No God to worship, and no fate to fear;
To me all Truth, and Faith, and Friendship seem,
The meteor lights and figments of a dream.
My vision fled, I can no more discern
A life to hope, a sacred Truth to learn;

Suns, worlds there are, and Beings wise and free,
But living Author, Father, none for me ;
Cold, heartless Fate, forever grinding, ground,
Lives, dies, revives, and chills creation round."

O leave, my son ! the rolling heavens above ;
Behold within a world of truth and love.
The living mind—a moving, shining sea,
With streams inflowing from Immensity.
Air, light, electric agencies supply
The touch, the taste, the curious ear, the eye,
Calm, conscious spreads the Intellect below,
Receives, secures the riches as they flow ;
We tread the plain, we climb the rocky steep,
And Time and Nature fill the inward deep.
Each glimpse, or murmur, swells the growing store,
Each year we count, and find the treasure more.
Fact, image, gathered from the world of sense,
The growing store we call Experience.
The work of Nature, work of man we know,
And learn what is the work of chance below.
We class, arrange, distinguish, understand,
The sign of Nature, sign of human hand ;
Imagination molds creations too,
All fictions these, and those we call the True.

But lo ! around, above that living sea,
A lustre shines from climes of purity ;
No door it needs, no window of the soul;
It comes unsought, and kindles up the whole.
Exalted, sparkling underneath the glow,
The troubled waters heave and move below :
In love and trust, each intellectual wave
Roils to the light, and leaves its silent cave,

And, blessing, hails the blessing from above,
So warm with life, so luminous with love.
Men called it Wisdom in Idumean clime,
"The Logos!" cried the sage of Olden Time,
But we, in lisping elements uncouth,
Have named the Light, Eternal Reason—Truth.
Bright Revelations from the world unseen,
We need not climb, or count the steps between;
They come, they pour their lustre on the deep,
Where shadowy forms in dim reflection sleep.
Disposed in brief triplicities, we find
Celestial Truths evolved from laws of mind;
Term under term, we may affirm, deny,
One formed in Nature, one beyond the sky.
Now both compared, the gift of sense may be,
Now both revealed, complete the mystic Three;—
And all we learn, and all we seek to know,
Three combinations bring to man below.

In vain we plunge the vortices among,
To suns remote, and mysteries unsung,
And climb, and soar the Universe around,
To find an Image which is ever found.
The true, the fair, the spiritual, the pure,
Illume the mind, and make its light endure.
A radiance fills the intellectual eye,—
Bright inward organ, with its inward sky;
It warms the soul, it lifts the bounding heart,
In all the heavens, of which we are a part.
Thus Reason, Sense, the inward store supply,
This from the world, that from beyond the sky;
Truth, Right, and Wrong the conscious soul conceives,
And Fancy paints, and reverent Faith believes.

We fondly deem that Beauty, Justice, Love,
Belong to earth, we see them not above.
With rolling Nature reels affrighted Sense,
And Reason whispers, "Hail Omnipotence!"
Light, Beauty, Order, Goodness from above,
And Reason breathes, "Omnipotence is Love!"
Green all the meads and blue the vaulted skies,
I hear within, "Omnipotence is Wise."
Song, gladness, plenty fill the field, the Wood,
I hear again, "Omnipotence is Good."
I hear from all that Duty calls to do,
The inward voice. "The Holy is the True."

"Enough! enough! I feel that smile again,
Warm from the deep, invisible domain,
A stream of light renews its sweet control;
The radiant visions sweep my kindling soul.
Unearthly forms in shining robes appear,
And heavenly sounds and symphonies I hear.
I see the pure, ethereal shapes of thought,
Stand forth with beaming lineaments inwrought.
I should have known no sun, or centre, far
In fadeless lustre of abyssmal star,
Reveals that Face in vestments of the True,
More beauteous than a shining drop of dew.
And yet the grand, the beautiful, the bright,
May stir the inward through the outward sight,
From worlds, so long in majesty mature,
The soul may reach the Perfect and the Pure."

May reach! and here the fond illusion lies;
May reach some orbless region of the skies!
May elevate the soaring soul to see
The Absolute in his Eternity;

Where angels sing and blissful spirits dwell,
Forever lulled on beds of asphodel;
The blest abode of some Aonian race,
In radiant height of Empyreal space!
As if the Good, the Absolute, the True,
Did not descend and dwell among us too;
As if this earth, a home to Adam given,
Were not a mansion and a part of heaven;
As if the soul must wander far away,
To find and feel the genial light of day!
Here Reason, Sense their antinomies find,
The shades and phantoms of imprisoned mind;
From age to age the same illusions play,
And this would nail, and that would woo away.
We soar aloft, and say we UNDERSTAND;
We count the stars when we should count the sand.
Fair Reason shines, revealing everywhere;
We live, and move, and have our being there.

Ye faithful stars! still watching as ye burn,
Time-honored dust in many a sacred urn,
Ye saw that dust, in dreamless slumber now,
Grow to be man, and crumble from his brow.
Ye saw him tread the vale, the moonlit hill,
Ye saw him pause, and start, and wonder still;
Raise his blue eyes to your ethereal flame,
And muse, and count, and kindle into fame.
If on the brow of Caledonian height,
He passed alone the thoughtful summer night;
Or in Ionia, or in Doris strayed,
Or far away by Indian hills delayed;
Ye saw him turn, and chase, and turn again,
Some fond ideal on his native plain,

Form, mold the mind of his believing age;
Ye see the dust of him we call, "The Sage."

In thought profound, one meditates alone;
His world within, the world he calls his own;
Beholds, reversed, the face of Nature there,—
Rocks, waters, woods, the sea, the crystal air.
There knowledge springs, here Faith and Hope begin,
The daughters, sons of images within.
There shower, and sun, and breeze, and beam prevail,
And seasons change, and passing storms assail.
A shadowy realm of light and darkness here,
Is all he sees, not all he finds to fear.
From youth to age, he gathers seed by seed,
Round, shadowy grains for Faith and Hope to feed,
And says, within this frame of breathing clay,
Thought, feeling, Truth, can come no other way;
A frame of dust, a soul of air and fire,
Material all, and all alike expire;
Since dissolution is the stern decree
Of fates that change, and fates that set us free;
Back to material elements we go,
Nor wake to feast, nor sleep to dream below.
Truth is the daughter of Experience,
Wrought into form from little seeds of sense;
And Wisdom but the weight of grain and gra'n,
That meet and swell, like mist in drops of rain.
For time and tide abrade the rolling dust,
Refine the heart and make the conscience just.
The soul of Numa, smooth about, above,
Harmonious atoms, rounded into love,
Will build the state, and make his people know
That Beauty is proportion here below;

K

That dearest friendships, sympathies of heart,
Are atoms meeting atomies apart ;
Joy, hope, remorse, devotion, love, desire,
Are radiant sparkles of commingling fire ;
And Gods, if Gods exist in climes unknown,
Like earthly men, are made of flesh and bone ;
Some Vulcan sledge the nail of Nature drove ;
Some peak Olympic props the throne of Jove.
This Universe is one eternal fall
Of raining atoms from the Crown of all,
Devoid of object, reason, aim, design ;
No hand beyond, no molding Will divine ;
A hungry, monstrous, moving, living mass,
Inhaling space, as we inhale a gas.

Enjoy, O man ! the sweets of land and sea ;
Thy heaven is sense, and earth is sense to thee.
Balmy the fragrant breeze of evening blows,
Luxurious Nature loves a soft repose.
Soft Lydian airs, Æolian voices sing
To every breath sweet thrills of pleasure cling.
Lo ! wanton Beauty walks the flowery vale,
Voluptuous joys are beckoning in the dale ;
Fly to the shades, the summer shades of love,
The earth is green, and heaven is warm above.
Or mount at dawn the flashing car of Time,
And catch the bliss that pours from every clime.
If long the night, the pause of pleasure long,
Lead up the dance, or drink the wanton song,
Or spread the feast, or drain the foaming bowl,
Falerian drops will warm the frigid soul.
Lo ! Nature bares her teeming breast to thee ;
This world is Venus, and thy heart is free !

"Abstain!" I hear the good Aurelian say,
"False smiles delude, and kisses will betray.
If every sense be but an inward sign,
Some floating phantom in that brain of thine;
If nerve and nature bring successive tides
Of watery vapor, where the soul resides;
If naught approach that deep, secluded throne,
But shadowy images of things unknown,
Why seek the bed, the board, the dance, the bowl?
What are these phantoms that beset the soul?
What all this whirling, warm, voluptuous scene,
These shades of Summer, and these vales of green?
Can these of bliss perennial fountains be?
You never taste them, and you cannot see.

Is pleasure but the thrilling of a nerve?
Why, then, a needle or a knife may serve.
How know that yonder smiling Fair is fair?
Where is the Image? In the brain, or there?
How can you know this Massic cup is sweet?
Can bowls, or beauties, reach the soul's retreat?
How vain the sounds, the sweets, the pleasures all,
The hands that beckon, and the smiles that call,
Green Summer vale, and warm, voluptuous sky,
And rosy lip, and passion-pleading eye!
Illusive dreams, from sun to shining sea,
Not blessed to be, they only seem to be!
Thy soul, amid the phantoms of a brain,
Allured to ruin, but allured in vain,
For even allurement is mere power to seem,
And ruin but an evanescent dream.
Dispel these Siren shadows that obtrude,
And reign the monarch of thy solitude.

Thy heart is thine; exert supreme control,
Blest ataraxia of impassive soul.
Pain, pleasure, sense are all delusive play;
Chase, mortal, chase these empty dreams away!
Assert thy proud prerogative, and be
The worthy shrine of lone Reality.

 Involved with misty images within,
Dover dares to doubt, yet fears it may be sin,
Probes nerve, probes brain, with keen and curious eye,
Proves faith a cheat, eternal Truth a lie;
Confused, perplexed, for homeless thought to find
A friendly roof in matter or in mind;
And now Idea from impression springs,
Now swells from naught, and makes the sum of things.
Vain visions all, for mere delusion shown,
Power, substance, cause, reality, unknown;
In nature now, and now within the brain,
Man seeks, pursues the dim abode in vain.
A spark—the sun! one deems them both the same,
A fluttering dream; a moth around the flame.
In vain the meads their aroma diffuse;
An inward phantom, not the mead, he views;
The moon commands the worship of the main,
The regal sun revolves the world in vain;
Moon, ocean, sun, a visionary whim,
A power unseen, can be no power to him.
Faith spins a circle, Truth an endless chain,
Each proof proposed demanding proof again.
Lo! Right and Wrong, lo! Good and Evil claim
Coequal honors in this polar frame.
No side espouse: seek neither that nor this;
Fair Ataraxia takes the genial bliss;

Man, Nature, God, of mortal visions wrought,
Man, Nature, God, evaporate in thought,
And Sextus, Fichte, Hume, and Hegel meet,
Four radiant thoughts, convened in space to greet.

"A gentle youth last term to Sydney came;
The Dean and Proctors seemed to dread his name,
E'en starch Professors stiffened in their prose,
When Milton's eye shone through the listening rows.
Yet he was mild, obedient, bland to all;
Assiduous, ardent, prompt at every call;
He "took the Board,"—he drew the diagram,
Air ever modest, brow forever calm;
There as he stood, with black and beaming eye,
We saw the wall, but he beheld the sky;
With ease instinctive, undelayed to learn,
His cusps and spirals knew which way to turn.
We read Alcestis, and his part alone,
Was made in tone, and word, and thought his own.
One day he made us shiver, as he read
The Grecian Heroe's mission to the dead:
"Within the sunless mansions I will go
Of Kora and the sable king below!
And I will plead, persuade the king to send
Alcestis to my hospitable friend,
The noblest man of this Thessalian land,
And I will place her blooming in his hand;
For, being noble, never shall he say,
He served a man too worthless to repay."
We seemed to hear the Hero in the youth,
His voice so breathed the glory of a Truth.

"Alone we wandered many a starry hour;
I loved him for his strange untutored power.

And once he said, when other themes were done,
"I saw you reading the Misopogon.
Erasmus, cased in these material days,
We sneer at Julian and the Orphic lays;
Believe me, friend, beneath these forms we see,
Shines all unseen the vast Reality.
This world is but a type of what we find,
Beyond the range of sensualistic mind.

"I know what holy contemplations do;
I have explored mysterious regions too;
Propitious hours of deep, abstemious thought,
The veil have lifted, and the visions brought,
These mortal walls, attenuate and thin,
Like gossamer, have let the lustre in;
And glorious hues invest the world around;
A tone unearthly thrills in every sound.
The trees, the hills approach me, and retire,
To endless azure runs the temple spire.
Then first emerge in all the vocal air
Symphonious hymns, expostulation, prayer;
Winds, waters, woods, become articulate;
Each motion murmurs words of fearful weight.
A pause ensues, a pause of strange delight,
With all the living universe in sight;
Oreads, and gnomes, and sylphs,—a dazzling train,
Come circling round me, visible and plain.
And though I lack the wisdom to command,'
They wait, they vanish, reappear, disband.
Yet still I feel this breathing coil of clay;
I see the human pageants of the day;
The powers of mind still hold a slight control,
Restrain, repress, incarcerate the soul,

But free at last, she leaps the mortal bound,
Springs to the worlds of Ecstacy profound.
Then wide before me, golden in the west,
Extend the radiant Islands of the Blest,
And happy spirits, rich in Truth divine,
With twinkling harps, along the meadows shine.
My soul exulting mingles in the train,
And talks with sages, charmed with Truth again.
Still further on, the Ministers of light
Stand clothed in smiles and robes of dazzling white;
Illustrious Powers, who made the world and man,
And still enlarge, perpetuate the plan ;
Still diving deeper in celestial Truth,
Blest with dominion and immortal youth.
And now I feel the influx of a Love,
Which draws resistless, draws me on above;
A conscious atom, burning in the sun,
I meet the blaze, and lose me in the One.
I live and hear the hymns of Olam sung,
I raise my voice, and find I have a tongue ;
I utter words of meaning not my own ;
The words, the truths roll thro' me from the Throne.
I need no light, I need no sun to see,
Within me lives and shines Eternity.
And I, a prophet, send my voice afar,
To listening sun and subeternal star."

 The fond enthusiast! lovely though he be,
No trusty guide, no polar star for thee.
Call Plato back to hold the golden rein,
And draw this charger from the clouds again.
Oh! mind! Oh, mortal! restless as the wave ;
No home but heaven, no requiem, but the grave.

Our flying hopes, now in the stream of sense;
Now beaming, star-like, in Omnipotence.
We chase some flitting butterfly of bliss,
Now cling to that, and now believe in this,
Now chase it there—look back, and seek it here,
Allured, deceived, by hope, and faith, and fear.
Blind tools of some insatiable desire,
We climb the stars, explore the central fire ;
We greet a gipsy from the land of Dates,
Full sure she sat in council with the Fates.
Far on the hill the green and gold begin ;
We lose the glory when we get within.
Away beyond the gray horizon rest,
Our Spirit-lands, our Islands of the Blest.
From shores remote we bring the healing balm,
Australian grass is good against the qualm !
Afar, afar ! the True, the Good, the Fair !
How false, how impotent our neighbors are !
We crowd, we call the traveler to tell,
Where wiser men, and fairer women dwell ;
Sigh as he talks of Sennaar or Nod,
Some Orient angel, or Hesperian God.
E'en Truth herself, a Wanderer Divine,
Must bring her lore from Ganges, or the Rhine,
Or set the soul from sense and reason free,
To fly abroad, and see as angels see !

 This fiery Monad, restive of restraint,
Beats round her cage, and flutters fierce or faint.
"O take, ye gods, these heartless walls away,
And let me triumph in celestial day!"
And yet she feels the pulse, recounts the breath,
And shrinks and shudders at the voice of Death.

Each ray, she thinks, admitted to her cell.
Has rapturous tales of liberty to tell,
She strives to climb the golden ray in vain,
Picks every cranny, tries each chink again.

Ah! could the soul from mortal bonds elope,
Run up the ray, and clear the azure cope,
Pierce, unadvised, the immaterial sphere,
Where spirits worship, and the Gods appear
What were she but a human soul at best,
A naked stranger startling all the Blest?
A speckled sprite of images and forms,
Of shower and sunshine, inundations, storms,
Of clouds and shadow, mountains, islands, seas;
Of wailing winds, and sighing symphonies!
How, as her wings the silent realm explore,
Assimilate her lore with angel lore!
Down from the steep, I see her look and sigh,
"My home! my earth! Away in yonder sky?
I lived in heaven, yet deemed I lived below,
From God and angels, doom'd to hopeless woe!
Ah, me! is not that ray the evening beam,
Warm, glowing, glancing from my native stream?
Oh, heaven! within that quarter of the sky,
What lovely vales of dear remembrance lie!
Familiar paths, with smiling Truth before,
I measured oft, and shall I tread no more?
Sure Nature holds no fitter spot to see
The charms of Beauty, smiles of Deity.
Let me return, regain my native sphere;
I see that heaven, that God is everywhere.
Let me return, with glad obedience wait;
The laws of Nature are the laws of Fate.

L

Sweet Resignation is the boon of bliss
Presumption blindly dares the last abyss.
The Father's house, a wide creation, calls.
His sons to meet and banquet in the halls.
The hand of Death will kindly lift the veil;
Some door for me will open to the gale.
Enough for me, if wafted to the shore,
I may again the gems of Truth explore,
In frame of earthly or celestial mold,
Enough to see new mysteries unfold.

Two living spheres inwoven make the whole ;—
The Sire of all, the never-dying soul.
Pure spirit that, and this a mingled state,
This prone to Evil, that Immaculate.
Let subject spirits in their functions know
Supreme above, subordinate below :
That matter rounds the surface of the sphere,
In which all less than Infinite appear.
Celestial bodies are but bodies still,
Devised by Wisdom, fashioned by a Will;
And all impassable the void between
The forms material and the Ens unseen.
Beyond the void, blue veiling as the sky,
The sacred Fields of Intuition lie ;
Thence, Power Divine creates, pervades the whole,
Gives form to matter, consciousness to soul.
Soul free, immortal, rational, divine,
If finite, bound in some material shrine.
The robes of Psyche ever float within
The vaults of night, and avenues of sin.
But who may tell how fine the Fates may draw
The threads of Hyle, ere they break her law.

Within, the sense of angel and of man,
Must probe, experience, not BEHOLD the plan,
Though sprinkling drops of Revelation flow
Bright from the Throne, refreshing worlds below.
Enough, to range the visible and see
The radiant Image of a Deity;
Enough, though finite, chained, immured, alone,
To feel the Logos beaming from the Throne;
Enough, to know the Right, to find the True,
The Infinite in glory, shining through;
Enough to see, and seeing, learn to know
Eternal Beauty mirrored all below;
Enough, to live and worship in the light
Of nameless Beauty, in the upper height;
With Love, and Truth, and Transport in the soul,
To see within an Image of the Whole.
Thus Plato saw, and found the voice to tell
The living waters of this inward well.
And though within the bounds of space and time,
The soul must rise to reach the true sublime;
Though ever, as unceasing ages flow,
A body binds and holds it down below;
Though all of pure, of heavenly, of divine,
Must pass a medium, and reflected shine,
Triumphant soul! uncircumscribed in this,
Thou art divine, canst have a taste of bliss!

   Immortal Essence, sigh no more to roam!
Behold how wide the universal home!
Thou hast the high, celestial boon to be;
Thy bosom draws the breath of Deity:
These waters murmur symphonies divine,
Sweet spirit tones in harmony with thine;

Delicious fruits are teeming from the earth,
On every side a new, mysterious birth.
The rose still sheds its fragrance on the gale,
The seeds of Eden bloom in every vale.
Truth, beauty, love, and hope, and memory dear,
And pressing hands, and kindred hearts are here.
The love, the truth, the sympathy the same,
As once, rejoicing, from the Father came;
All swell thy being with the light to know,
That heaven above has made a heaven below.
Why seek Creation's central fire to find,
Some world of light congenial with the mind;
Why range the gathering galaxies remote,
In shadowy realms impalpable to float?
Why, even there, in supercosmal day,
Thou hast the tinge and temperament of clay.
Why, even there, on impious wing decoyed,
Thou hast no pinion for the senseless void;
There unapproached, the Absolute unknown,
Throbs through the veil of images alone.

Fanatic Priest, whose star is in the brain,
Thy fires explore Futurity in vain!
Blind Flamen, leave thy visionary shrine.
No victim slain can pass the bourne divine;
No savory odor reach the viewless shore,
No bleeding virgin bear thy message o'er.
What miracles believing souls might do,
Could faith in system make the system true!
Thou hast believed; and mountain, river, sea,
Have teemed with wrangling deities for thee;
Strange exultations swelled thy heaving frame,
And clouds withdrew, and tones prophetic came;

Old Earth unbarred her stony gates below,
Avernian groves, and myrtle shades of woe;
Styx, Phlegethon, and lakes of penal fire,
Disease, and Age, and Shapes, and Gorgons dire,
And Death, and Discord wild, and Toil, and Fear,
And Lethe there, and dread Cocytus here;
The Elm of Dreams, a dream to every leaf,
And vengeful Cares, and iron-beds of Grief,
With distant vision of Elysian plains,
Beyond the pools of penalties and pains.
Thine altars, temples, Pythian shrines I see,
The world is all one Pantheon for thee;
Priest, Pontiff, Augur, awe the timid throng,
And mystic Sybils bear thy books along;
The sacred Vestals guard thy fadeless fire;
The victim bleeds, the holocausts aspire;
The veil is drawn, and lo! the coming years,
The looming fate of centuries appears;
The vital streams of hecatombs must flow,
If heaven may flourish, or the gods may grow.

 In far Judea drops a viewless seed;
A change invades the spirit of thy creed;
A Power unseen reforms the atmosphere;
Thy altars fall, thy temples disappear;
Thy impious axe administers the blow;
The cheek of huge Serapis rings below.
E'en thou, recoiling in the breach between
The past Belief and Destiny unseen,
Didst hold thy hand, a moment pause to see
If Jove or Christ be Lord of land and sea.
Then came the songs of Zion down the vale;
The deserts rang; the mountains breath'd the tale;

New temples rose, new anthems filled the air,
And lone recesses uttered praise and prayer.
The gods were gone; the land, the sky were free;
And hermit Truth sat by the hearth with thee.

  Alas, for thee! Alas, for Truth divine!
The storms are creatures of the beams that shine:
And thou didst creep, with all thy holier lights,
Through filthy cells, to frame monastic rites;
To dream dark dreams, fantastic visions tell,
And liquify a drop of blood, to sell;
To light thy tapers in the blaze of day;
To scrape white bones, and kneel at tombs to pray;
Thy vigils, fasts, conventicles to hold;
Thy walls to hang with eyes and feet of gold,
Till old Didona and the Pythian shrine,
Might sneer at worship so debased as thine,
And jarring Synods find it hard to say,
If Grace had come, or Truth been chased away.

  Alas! if Truth, the heavenly and the pure,
Could dwell with councils and with priests secure!
Is there no shrine within the azure sphere,
No tempered brain, no loving heart sincere,
Whence sacred streams from age to age may flow,
Nor meet nor mingle with the mire below?
The gem matures its lustre in the mine,
Though rayless mass and muculence confine.
The shell reposes fadeless in the sea;
Why not, O man, the shining Truth in thee?
Alas, for man, the Bard hath lived and sung,
With drops of glory dripping on his tongue;
Hath seen the living wheels that roll afar,
From Nature's God to Nature's eldest star;

Hath caught the gleams of Immanence supreme,
Like veins in marble, piercing through his dream;
Celestial white with opal lines besprent, —
Eternal Truth and earthly shadows blent.
Yes, all beneath that river of the True,
Whence Homer, Burns, their inspiration drew,
Sweet Revelations float in light along
The murmuring curves and cadences of song,
Till Homer, Burns, in ecstacy would start,
With burning raptures flashing through the heart;
Till bards and men, in dreamy lapse forget,
The drop Divine in forms material set.

Nor these alone have sigh'd or sung in vain;
The Prophet sounds the living Word again.
The open visions rise and re-appear:
Strange invocations rouse the dreaming Seer,
And Shiloh hears the child's reluctant tale,
With tingling ears and melancholy wail.
A Prophet walks the plains of Palestine,
His forehead lighted from the world unseen,
And fiery tongues of inspiration still,
Pervade Esdraelon and its holy hill.
Through the brown copses, down the smoky dale,
The Prophet hastens, trembling, haggard, pale;
The burden of the Infinite he feels;
The thunder talks melodious peals on peals;
And speaking winds, and hum of weeping leaves,
And cloud that rolls, and mountain top that heaves.
Upon his lip descends the living coal;
The Urim of the Lord within his soul;
He asks of heaven no seraph wing to fly
Above the gates that open to his eye;

The Holy One descends upon the hill;
He swims the Glory, as the valleys fill;
Within his breast, the fountains of a well,
Gush up in judgments which his tongue must tell;
And frantic with the burden of his love,
He utters wisdom only known above.
He sees the tents of Cushan in distress,
The Lord revealing from the wilderness.
The mountains scatter and the vales expand;
The curtains wave along the Midian land.
The voiceful waters lift their hands on high,
The sun in worship, pauses in the sky,
The prophet's footstep on the sands we see;
His voice is still: but read his legacy,
God's Truth that flash'd in lightning thro' his heart;
We kiss, adorn, parade her for the mart!
Oh, Faith! is faith a mockery, or a dream?
Do we believe and worship, or blaspheme?
Does Symbol, Creed, Analogy deceive
This formal, cold belief that we believe?

A trifle is it? I have power to know
This Masorah of wisdom sent below!
This Seed prophetic of celestial green;
This Arc, expanding into skies unseen,
Whence hopes immortal plume their wings to soar
The endless Spiral that returns no more!
The Prophet meets me, and amazed I see,
His words unfolding into history.
Dim grows the sunlight, dim the starry ray,
They pale to mingle with my locks of gray;
But rays I find within this holy page,
Whose lustre dances on the brow of age.

Bathed in the Light, I too become a Seer;
Deep visions from the Inner Shrine appear.
And though I may not tear myself away
From shapes, and forms, and images of clay;
And though forever o'er my head expand
The shadow and the terror of a Hand,
I bless the terror, hide me in the Love;
I know a Light celestial shines above.
If dust abused the power to disobey,
I know that Mercy took the boon away;
That man, unfaithful, lost the link divine,
And tore from Nature all his tainted line;
That Justice weighed, and Mercy wept to gain
Annihilation for eternal pain;
That Nature thundered, deep, from sky to sky;
"The soul that sinneth, dying, it shall die,"
And from the day, and from the soul untrue,
The tainted boon of Endless Life withdrew;
I hear a Voice through Nature's dark domain,—
"My Life, a ransom, Man shall live again!"

A soft, warm bosom folds Eternal Truth;
Eternal Wisdom springs to golden youth;
Dark Nature feels through all her glad domain
The living pulse of Deity again.
The soul refilled, as morning fills the dew,
Wakes with its own eternity in view;
The Dead obey the voice of God within
The murmuring tombs and catacombs of sin;
The blushing dust with life begins to burn;
It feels the glad Divinity return.
First dew of Light untreasured by the sun,
Beneath the vaults of pleading Nature won,

M

And Nature feels the First-Out-shining Beam
Light on the hills, the ocean, and the stream.

   He breathed the air;—the air hath life to give,—
He touched the wave, and all the waters live.
Floats all abroad the garment of the King;
The earth exults, the heavens responsive ring.
Ethereal verdure walks the vales along;
I hear the mountains breaking into song;
The soul rewakens to primeval love,
Renewed, reborn from elements above.
And feels her immortality again
Rekindling down the universal chain.

   "Oh, listen, father!—We are not alone;
Some voice beguiles the pauses of your own;
Like evening airs among Æolian pines,
A soft, voluptuous mystery entwines,
And moves in mazy iteration sweet,
Along the sacred wonders you repeat."

   I hear it often; happy now to see
That other ears may drink the symphony.
It seems some chord of music in the brain:
You speak a truth; it speaks that truth again:
Its breathings gush like fountains in a well.
Without, within the soul, you cannot tell.
Now in the cloud, now in the cave profound;
You feel the truth before you hear the sound.
It speaks sweet mysteries, destinies unknown,
And yet the tone, the language seems your own.
I hear it now. I kneel, melodious Power!
Kneel! my Erasmus. Holy is the hour!

THE VOICE:

His ways of old the Lord reveals to man
His ways of old, before the world began!
I heard his voice awake the dewy morn,
I went beside him when the day was born.
Before the spirit brooded the abyss,
I was anointed in the realms of bliss;
Before the gray antiquity of Time,
I meted all the limited sublime.
I went before him, like an only child,
When Love and Truth imparadised the Wild.
I drew the Plan ye have not failed to see,
This cubic poise of order and degree.
I rule the play of agent, element,
Make true the centre, mass, equipolent,
Till kindling sun and rolling world became,
A thing of glory; one harmonious frame,
And Nature sent her Eldest Born to try,
The spiral paths and orbits of the sky.

To fill my plan in regions far away,
New worlds are made, and systems framed to day;
And long ago, did angels hail the birth,
Of sun and moon, and your maternal earth.
I stood before him, day, celestial day,
As Beauty came, and chaos passed away;
I saw his hand the winds and waves prepare,
Unwrap the Haraphel of land and air,
Ensphere the light, and raise the azure hill.
And send abroad the river and the rill.
I tuned the air to sweetest melody,
I twined the morning beam of colors three;

I edged the clouds with gold and crimson hue,
I robed the vales with green, the sky with blue,
Bade fountains gush from every mountain side,
To lawn and vale the living streams supplied.
Then vernal bloom and sylvan glories came,
And blushing buds of every hue and name,
And fruits delicious, clustering on the tree,
A thousand forms of fresh fertility.
O, had you trod my primitive domains,
Where fruits spontaneous load the teeming plains,
Where all in peace and purity around,
Progressive Nature verges to her bound,—
Those ancient heavens I saw him first prepare,
Where nobler beings breathe maturer air,
Ye might discern, could dust endure to see
The scope of Nature's glorious destiny.

There sweeping flood and central fire have done,
Their last behest for satellite and sun;
Pacific waters feel the storm no more,
Nor fierce convulsions heave the peopled shore.
There cultured hills in gentle slope ascend,
Sweet islands bloom, and continents extend,
And greener meads rejoice with fairer flowers,
And woodland raptures always fill the bowers,
And wholesome airs immortal fragrance bring,
And spirits meet you, on the friendly wing.
For worlds mature, their elements refined,
Receive high souls, to riper climes assigned,
And forms celestial, wrought of holier clay,
May tread the plain, or wing the golden day.

Thus Nature rises, regions thus designed
To feed, to fill the glad, immortal mind;

Thrones, Powers, Dominions, down to distant Man;
For this the suns, for this the worlds began.
Love, Beauty, Truth, the elements supply,
But every false, unfaithful soul must die.
From impious hearts I take the Truth away,
And all their Beauty and their Love decay;
With these I sow the air, the earth, the main,
And living dust is made to breathe again;
Till, gathering life from breeze, and stream, and ray,
The new-born Essence takes some nobler way,
No drop descends upon the hills in vain,
All Nature labors through her vast domain;
No idle grain is swept into the sea,
No leaf unpurposed trembles on the tree;
These atoms all shall reach the distant goal,
In proud delight to incarnate a soul,
Till raptured Beings, deep in bliss shall find,
The aim of Matter passing into Mind;
Till all the dust of all the worlds shall be
Refined, relumed with immortality.
Life, Death, the Good, the Evil, all conspire,
To fill the Anthem, harmonize the Choir.

 All are my servants;—I have taught them all;
I speak, they go; they hasten when I call.
I see, I hear, in this stupendous frame,
Each earnest soul; I know each humble name.
The vast procession widens on my view,
From Nature's heart, to Nature's faintest blue.
They rise through perils, toil through pains to learn
The Love, the Truth that makes the Seraph burn.
Each rising, leaves his dust at every stage,
To robe the spirit of some wiser age,

Elijah thus his vestments left behind;
A wiser Prophet walked among mankind.

   They study Truth and Virtue as they go;
What friendship is, what sympathy, they know:
And toiling long, they reach the plains serene,
To add the wisdom which they found between.
Priest, Poet, Prophet, led from sphere to sphere,
Who learned their elements of wisdom here,
Grasp now with ease far visions of the True,
And play with mysteries undream'd by you.
Seers, sages, sovereigns, from the worlds afar,
Whose morning Sun was your remotest star,
Till deep with blissful Kedoshim we soar,
Where dust dissolves and sorrows flow no more,
Where they can gaze on sky and central sun,
And taste the bliss of glorious labor done.

   We treasure there the Truth ye cannot see;
That pain is handmaid of felicity;
That tears are jewels; Death the silken veil
Which hides the angel till the mortal fail;
That soul must, in the powers of Nature, fill
Nine Avatars alternate Good and Ill,
Ere tried, refined, in thought and feeling pure,
She find her Immortality secure.
Most sweet is joy when sorrow lingers still;
Ye cannot know the Good without the Ill.
The heavens are bluest when the storm is by;
I make the gulf, to make you love the sky;
And nurtured thus, this moral world within
The forms of clay, vicissitude, and sin,
In bright procession, moves from height to height,
From Nature's verge to Nature's Central Light.

All finite souls are limited to see
The partial Truth, within their own degree;
Yet ever opens to the rising view,
The loftier springs and fountains of the True.
From skies and waters, wilds and woodlands here,
Ye fondly paint each old and older sphere;
Ye hear the music of the hill, the bower,
And deem your air hath ALL melodious power:
Ye study forms and images divine,
And think no clearer images can shine.
Oh! ye shall feed, if still your faith endure,
On Truth indeed, on Beauty high and pure;
Celestial bodies shall be yours, to range
The slopes and summits of eternal change;
And as ye walk the plains of brighter day,
Your strange delusions softly melt away,
Ye sigh no more for weary souls to lie,
All disembodied in some quiet sky,
In dreamy bliss, reposing with the blest,
In lazy visions of eternal rest.

God loves to work; and yours the bliss to bear,
His high behests from listening sphere to sphere;
Glad messengers, with Truth upon your wing,
To distant worlds his revelations bring;
And talk with seers and sages, who shall be
The light of Olams in eternity;
Yes even walk these renovated bowers,
Where men shall live of more exalted powers,
And richer strains of poesy and song
The glorious theme of Love and Truth prolong.
For knowledge, like the waters of the sea,
Shall fill and feed the nations yet to be.

Vain superstitions from your hearts dispel;
The Lord of Nature knows his purpose well.
Material frames must evermore invest;
The finite soul must throb within a breast.
Be true, be faithful, manly, generous, wise;
Meet Death rejoicing: Nought but Evil dies.
The soul matured for Nature's higher sphere,
Must try nine zones of Good and Evil here.
Shrink not; your heart will beat with me again;
Heed no delusions; mortal fears are vain.
Your fate, your life are hid in God with me;
Lay down your dust; the Truth shall make you free;
And radiant dust shall once again impole
The Incarnation of a faithful soul.
Then ye shall learn, with rapture deep and strange,
That Principles eternal never change;
That Life and Goodness, Virtue, Patience, Love,
Though shadows here, are verities above;
That every soul must see the PLAN complete,
Where Hope and Memory, Truth and Mercy meet;
That Nature hath no funeral pile to fear;
That heaven's last thunder none shall ever hear.

IDOTHEA.

II

GOOD AND EVIL.

Ἀλήθεια δὴ πάντων μὲν ἀγαθῶν θεοῖς
ἡγεῖται πάντων δὲ ἀνθρώποις.
Plato.

The True, the Good, existing as attributes, imply the existence of a Necessary Being. In the Infinite they become identical. A positive variable Attribute, passing through the Infinite, becomes a negative Reality. Hence, in finite Experience, much that is False and Evil must be found. Some of them traced and compared.

MORE LOVE!

"LET THERE BE LIGHT."—That light was Love,
Unfolded from the gates above;
For Love was but the Light unborn,
Till Darkness opened into Morn.
Before Hyperion's golden flame,
From heaven the rosy Eros came,—
The Dove divine,—the Grace to give
This dust to breathe, this heart to live;
The harmony of heart with heart,
The whole encompassing the part,
The part embosomed in the Whole,
And all pulsating with a soul,
Responsive, throbbing—breast to breast;
The Dove that blesses and is blest;
The Love that lives within the Light,
With dear delights of sound and sight;
That paints the plain, that vaults the sky,
Attunes the ear, enchants the eye,
And calls the kindling soul to be
A living, leaping ecstasy,
Forever panting for the More
Which fills the Lord's celestial store.

Then Beauty—Daughter of the True,
Stooped to the range of mortal view,
And Love, benevolent, divine,
First taught these beauteous worlds to shine,
The flowers to wear ethereal hue,
The vale be green, the mountains blue,

And Venus flew from cloud to wave,
Rejoicing in the bliss she gave;
Up sprung the pulse of Love and Feeling,
With voice and tongue to dust appealing:

"Be wise, be vigilant, be true;
Love may diverge to Hate in you;
Pride, glory, power, wealth, passion, strife,
May steep in Crime the Good of life,
And Evil—Eblis of the Crime,
Embitter all the streams of time.
And clashing tongues shall writhe with hate,
And bleeding bosoms talk of Fate,
And fetters stained with blood shall be
The bitter prize of Purity."

"I have not loved the world,"—and why?
The wounded heart bedims the eye,
And o'er the Grace of Nature throws
The gory drapery of its woes.

Oh! haste the day, devolving Fate,
When man shall find no crime to hate:
My Love, my Dove, come haste away:
Bring from the hills the brighter day,
When Love, the complement of Law,
Shall yield no troth and trust for awe.
Lo! now the paths of God are straight:
The heart, with angels at the gate,
Shall feel the Love which makes the Fair,
Warm in the universal air,
And crime, remorse, and hate shall be
The fading verge of Memory.

GOOD AND EVIL.

Idyl I.—Eudæmonia.

Up yonder slope ascending from the stream,
Whose pearly eddies lave its verge of gray,
To hail the rosy morning on the steep,
Where furze and hazel copses teem around,
And willows broad, tall sycamores extend
Their leafy boughs, like arms, athwart the Smith,
How sweet to wander when the heart was calm,
And Peace and Virtue dwelt amid our homes!
The lovely Smith, how smooth the limpid flow,
Meandering as he moves along, and darts
His sparkling glances, quickly dancing round,
In joy to meet the morning's temper'd ray,
And, stealing through the foliage green and glad;
The sylvan waves with glittering gems of gold,
Haste onward to the briny sea afar!

A little further up the growing green,
An humble cottage stands between the herds
Bovine, stout, bulky, fat among the trees:
A cottage meek as that of Bethany;
Where far from busy life, in sweet content,
How oft we sat, to see the sun go down,
And laugh to hear the zealous whippoorwill!
How oft we strayed yon devious forest walk,
Along the path where parasitics creep,
And saw Apollo rising from his couch
To give the glory of a new-born day!

The brightening clouds stood, waiting at his throne,
Abashed and blushing till they stole away.
The early songsters tried their hymns again,
In ecstacy to hail the Lord of life ;
And buds, and leaves, and flowers of countless hues,
With deeper tints imbibed, awoke and smiled.

We fed no fond illusions. On the Past
We often mused, when hill and narrow plain,
And sunny slope, that shields us from the storm.
A hunting-ground for savages remained.
E'en from the echoing shore of old Atlantic,
Would Fancy lead us o'er the wilds to tread
The rocky coast Balboa sealed with toil,
And stood amazed, as like an endless sheet,
The watery Eden spread before his gaze.
All this, by Nature's hand in native wealth
Arrayed, stood waiting for the plow.
These breezy valleys, slopes, and mountain sides,
With fragrance sweet, of deep-hued vernal bloom,
Which would have charmed the muse of Solomon,
When chanting her voluptuous song of love,
She hovered o'er the consecrated Vale
Of Sharon. In those early days, a vast
Unpenetrated Night of forest shade
Was here the haunt of howling monsters still.
Yonder sparkling rill, which dances fairy-like
Along the sunny vale, with laughing glance,
Whispering to Touch-me-nots and Cresses green,—
"Refresh yourselves, and beautify my path,"—
In joyous freedom glides along in light,
To bear its wavy tribute to the sea.
But then unseen, it wound its sunless path,

Leaping the deep ravine with gurgling speed,
And hurrying round the cliff plunged in the vale.
Its darksome way more lazily discerned,
It drank the secrets of the vocal oaks,
As to the clouds and Western winds they sighed;
There lingering in the quiet solitude,
Till glad again it caught the sky-lark's notes.
As echoing through the foliage dense they rose
And towered in warbling cadence o'er the moor;
Then stealing softly through the copses dark,
With the hard pebbles paused in colloquies.
With patient hunger the king-fisher gazed,
Sustained by hope, its crystal bosom through,
And peered, and waited for his evening prey.

And now the blue-jay pipes his glad return
With puny trumpet o'er the echoing hills,
From Selvas of the sunny land of birds.
The golden robin flashed his nimble glance
Like lightning flickering in the caverns deep;
And traced the brook, as babbling on it went.
Down by Akosa's wicker lodge it passed,
And turned abruptly by a crumbling trunk,
Then creeping round in search of some egress,
It caught within the mirror of its breast
Two images and gently held them there:
Sweet treasure, happy pair! two dusky loves,
Transported, buoyant in each other's joy,
Though rustic as the log on which they sat.
Wild as the rugged cliffs and rocks they roam'd,
But true as Nature's faithful law could be.
Each word poetic, naked, unadorned,
Unvarnished talk, no doubting cloud between,

As the sweet lore of ardent feelings breathed
Into her timid ear.   The breeze that fann'd
Her blushing cheek less dulcet than her breath;
Her heart untickle as the dewy star,
Now smiling through the net of tangled boughs,
Along the eddy twinkled its assent;
Confiding as the infant on the breast,
Fair IROQUOIS accepted the embrace
Of WAWATAM, nor doubted he the pledge.
With them deceit and falsehood had no name;
Duplicity and guile had never touched
Their artless souls.   Simplicity was love.
As Adam waking from his lonely dream,
With joy ecstatic ran to meet the spouse,
His other self, the queen of Paradise,
So WAWATAM, his lofty brow elate,
Clasped to his heart the lovely IROQUOIS.

How often, in the night of crusted snow,
When bent beneath his load of mountain game,
His locks of jet all frosted with the storm,
His stalwart limbs exhausted in the chase,
Did WAWATAM, the monarch of the wild,
Pursue his pathless way along the hills,
And as his step grew heavier, swell'd his soul
With cheerful thoughts of home.   High beat his heart,
For soon beneath his sacred wicker roof,
Beside the glowing embers, prince-like, him
Regaling with his calumet, his We-weens all,
Would throng around with smiling eye and face.
Reclining there in magisterial ease,
He bids his faithful IROQUOIS prepare
The rich repast with fingers swift for joy.

He sees her face so patient, so serene,
Content to serve the monarch like a slave,
And yet the service be her joy alone.
There little rustics sit, their faces glad,
Bright sparkling eyes that watch the savory joint,
The steaming spit turned by the happy Guh.
First Ooskwaun with ample bit she cheers,
Laughing the words Papoos Kegaguwap.

And oft on yonder knoll, beside the beech,
We sat and watched the tide of time go by,
Marked by old Phœbus, on his daily toil;
Adown the West he hastens to his couch,
And dips into the distant sea of blue.
The golden clouds with crimson blushes glowed,
Amid the radiance of his hallow'd brow,
Hung o'er his steep descent, and gazed afar,
Watching to see him greet the Ocean Isles.
Then old Sylvanus hushed the chorister,
The pious wood-choirs their Sopranos ceased,
And the plain, humble dwellers of the pond,
With jarring force their croaking organs tried.

And now 'twas in the time of golden grain,
We saw the peasants hasten o'er the field.
How pleasing, when the Reapers of the day
With faithful toil have dress'd the harvest field,
That each may seek a home of quiet rest,
And meet the greeting of a happy face!
The babe in transport climbs his weary knee,
And lisps in language soothing to the heart.
The nectar sweet of industry he sips
Before the frugal board. The chemist finds
No such Elixir in his crucibles:

O

Boon of the good, the gift of love to men:
Plain virtue keeps a shrine, and there to kneel
Is not the lot of conquerors and kings.

And yonder up the hill, broad, green with trees,
Go winding herds of oxen, richly fed
By Nature's generous bounty, calves and cows,
All buoyant in the playfulness of life,
Called by the gentle voice of fair Elaine.
And now a volume of melodious tones,
Poured forth from her delicious lips, enchants
The neighboring hills, and lends the evening air,
A most delicious burden for the ear.
Responsive echoes waken in the hills,
And earth exults to find the angels here.
The lovely nymph, unconscious of herself,
Trips fairy-like along the stony path.
Her golden curls, like sunbeams through the shade,
Play with the zephyrs, and her brow upturned,
Betrays the tracery of unspoken love.
I cannot tell how beautiful she was,
Nor half the witchery of that soft, blue eye.
Her voice was like the sweet harmonic tone,
Drawn from the chord by some unearthly touch.
The Arab robber, or the beggar child,
All would have felt that meaning voice alike.

Erasmus met her, and his days became,
A new enjoyment. Yet they never spoke,
In passing, many months; but o'er her brow
There stole a light which was not of the sun;
And he with softer step pursued his way,
And seemed afraid to let her think he saw.

Her origin unknown to all but one,

And he around it nursed a mystery ;
The homeless Waif some friendly hand had found,
And sought a shelter in this other Vale.
Her wondrous beauty, growing as she grew,
Unfolded in the light of yonder halls,
And all these hills became a new delight.
The fairy stranger often loved to tell
Of Mundleville, the lucid stream beside.
The mother who had stood her in the flags,
Had stepp'd aside, and never come again.

Meanwhile, in blissful contemplation wrapt,
Each morn and eve she visited the fields,
Driving her charge along the rustic lane ;
And often paused to view the humble walls,
Where young and ardent met the bloom of youth.
Those walls so dear to many, call us still
And send our memory back to happy days,
More dear because our happy days are few.

MUSÆUS.

Old House, I love thee ! proudly, fondly turn
My earnest gaze upon thy time-worn walls.
Things are the signs of thought ; and all thy parts
Make up the history of my happy youth.
What heart, that true to noble impulse, beats,
Can e'er forget youth's happy, joyous time,
When life was but a play-day, and he knew
No care or guile, for it was full of truth.
We parted long ago, and yet the heart,
When wandering o'er the vistas of the past,
As Noah's raven to the Ark returned,
Comes back to thee, and finds a safe retreat.

Here stood the proud old Roman, here the Greek,
With flashing eye, and heart all full of song.
Here Mathematics paced with solemn tread,
And here light Muses gayly tripp'd along;
Here stern Philosophy, with kindling face,
Lean'd musing of himself. And there He sat,
That gifted man, moving them to his will.
His friends were mine, and they were noble friends,
Fit for a soul as ardent as his own.
But Yesterday, they were in jovial mood;
To day they sleep, and when will they awake!
Oh! there is now a deep and conscious want,
A pain of emptiness within these walls!

As musing thus, one night beneath the moon,
Half-dreaming Fancy, morbid with regret,
Lent lips and language to the dear old walls:
"Time flies, Musaeus! Sad behest of Fate,
To deal to man and earth eternal change.
Bare walls, and benches, silence, stirless air,
Alone were mine, until a Bion came,
And filled me with his friends. For he was kind;
All are not thus. He left, I know not why,
It may be Envy called her hideous brood
Which stand like shadows in the lanes of life.
It may be yellow, worthless dross that gave
Regret to me, and silence to my friends.
Oh! I could wish these rugged walls away!
But let me watch his glorious treasures here,
And wait in patience for his glad return."

Then silence fell, and with it sadness came
Upon my spirit, as I deeply mused;
Perchance, my friend had reason to be grave,

Since pleasure lost, is but a kind of pain.

BION.

 Fond of mutation ; dreaming of the More,
I find me here amid these quiet homes.
And now each morn first opens to my view
A clustering circle of retired abodes—
A fairy range of nut-brown cottages—
I tread forgotten paths, and feel once more,
Fresh ties, with softness of the silken cord,
Linking my heart with strangers. O, to me
A friendly greeting is a boon divine ;
To mark, as here, warm sunlight on the brow ;
To clasp the ready hand, and read the smile
Of kindly welcome beaming on the day.
Cold Stoic! This a world so full of gloom?
I see, I see!—long may the bliss endure,—
From field below to golden cloud above,
Blest radiance of the Beautiful abroad :
The rosy Morn that lifts her crimson lid,
Kissing yon hill in whispers with the sky ;
The copse, the corry, mead, and level lawn,
With all their garniture of grass and leaf ;
The gilded spire, the glittering dome below :
Westward the mass of human dwellings looms,
Marshall'd in broad diversity around,
Each sheltering there rich stores of home-felt joy,
Some tie invisible of love untold,
Hopes, wishes, fears, refined beatitudes,
Those charms unseen that cluster round the hearth,
Which knit our souls, and link them with the skies.
There cheerful mothers smile contentment round,
And blooming damsels grace the gay saloon ;

And bright-eyed boys, and rosy laughing girls,
Sport in the halls and throng the corridors.

Lo, yonder! on that sunlit summit fair,
Midst gladsome beams and zephyrs stealing by,—
Those whispering Ariels who commune with man,
If man's impetuous heart would pause to learn,—
There stand the stately walls I hope to fill
With spirits ardent for the Sage's crown;
Young, soft, immortal bosoms, formed to feel
The genial thrill of universal Truth,—
That warm pulsation, which with spirit force,
Cleaves the abysmal solitudes of space,
Teaching far earth deep mysteries of life.
Come, generous youth! aspiring genius, come!
Let us await thee, with the hallow'd ray,
Of star-born science, and the lore of Eld.
Come, let me intertwine, with new delight,
Her radiance with the garlands of thy brow.
Come, let us reason; and each tingling nerve
Shall feel each day the touch Ithuriel.
Come, share this reciprocity of bliss,
Which lends the soul development of power.
Sensation, Fancy, Reason, Taste refined,
Shall come in streams of loveliness and light,
O'er all our lucid lapse of studious hours.
O, come, and let us talk with sages old;
Minds that have made Antiquity a mine;
Plato, and Homer, and the awful voice
Which roll'd beneath the Macedonian throne.
Come, let us tune the Doric reed again,
Recall Sicilian shepherds to the fold;
Triumph with Pindar, or with Moschus moan.

Or let us hie to sweet Italia's clime,
And con the classic minstrelsy of Rome;
Descend with Dante, or with Tasso soar,
Bewail the lost, or free the Holy Land.
Or if thy taste allure thee to the shade,
Where Nature plies her alchemy unseen,
Come, let us listen to her lessons too,
And learn the wisdom of her wondrous fame,
Peruse amazed, her hieroglyphic vaults,
The mysteries of her ever-changing forms,
Her subtle essences, her forces, powers,
Her strange affinities, aversions, births :
Or mount the starry arches of the night,
Trace mingling orbits, count revolving suns
Record their phases, magnitudes, and paths,
Pass suns and systems, and devoutly feel,
The sacred awe of higher, holier stars.

   All these have language, if we hear aright,
And learn to read the Alphabet of heaven.
Trees have their voices, wandering winds their lore ;
Kind Nature writes her prophecies on leaves,
And stones can utter sermons to the wise.
Come, then, bright youth, and let us learn to heed
The meaning and the mystery revealed
Through every sense that stirs the conscious mind,
And we shall love each other with enduring joy,
And time, and change, and age, and envious Ill,
Shall but refine the flavor of our bliss.
What are the raptures of voluptuous ease,
Of wealth, of crowns imperial, when compared
With whispers in the fountains of our loves?
The voice of Science breathing in the heart,

Defining Beauty, Goodness, Justice, Law.
The Wisdom, in this universe of things,
Forever stealing from the rolling spheres,
In language not of earthly syllables;
But dropping, like an elemental smile,
From soul to soul in kisses of sweet joy?

GOOD AND EVIL.

Idyl II.—Nemesis.

Bright Summer mornings, with their diamond dews,
Lawns sleeping in their garniture of green,
And windy wilds, and vales of fragrant mead,
Loquacious meads that dally with the sun,
And roaming herds, and flocks upon the hill,
All these congenial, swell the pious soul
With sense of boundless, free benevolence ;
I feel a soothing pulse of thankfulness,—
Intuitive responses to the Good.
Oft Friendship comes, and goes with smiling brow :
I love the touch of warm and welcome hand :
Kind heaven has studied every genial art,
To touch this world with gleamings from beyond ;
But Sorrow is the dearest friend to me :
Sage Melancholy, musing at the spring,
O'er tender partings, losses of the Dear !
I thank ye, heavens, that such be in the world.
These drops are sweeter than the joy of smiles :
Tears, sighs, regrets, have sanctified this air,
Have made the forest holy. Earth and sky,
Stream, mountain—Mentors for the inward world—
Are consecrated with the bliss of tears.
I love the Earth—dear, faithful Earth :—

She is divine; she has so many tombs.
In her warm bosom sleeps the loveliest face!
This Air, sweet Air! still keeps the dearest voice,—
The voice which called me Arionel; heard once,
She said, in vision far away from Earth.
Then did I take sweet elements of sound,
In dreams she taught me; from Elaine they made
Lorraine, which, day and night, this air repeats!
Sweet air, thou art so very dear to me!

The wail of ages lives upon the breeze!
Old threnodies have charmed the Tragic muse;
I love to weep in her melodious woe.
Castalian sorrows feed the pensive heart,
And steep it in the luxury of grief,
Old banquets feast me now, by day and night:
For I am lonely; and the choral Muse
Hath found the secret of voluptuous pain.
Ionian sorrows harmonize with mine,
Prometheus and the Suppliants weep with me;
The solemn, mystic, strong Euphorides
Sends forth the wail of Gods from dim Eleusis;
The Danean daughters, and the Trojan Dames,
Orestes and Electra, steeped in tears,
A feast for Sorrow in her twilight shades.
Harmonious numbers poured from Colone,
The ancient men of Salamis and Athens,
Sad weepers wailing for the son of Pæan.
And he of tenderest soul, the child of Pathos,
Whose choral song was laved in love and tears;
Himself an exile, born at Salamis,
Calls forth the Argive Dames, and Theseus forth,
In suppliant woe, the eloquence of Eld.

Is not this world in sympathy with me?
The ages all? The years send forth a wail.
From bleak Siberia, where in exile, too,
The son of Weimer weeps the lot of man;
Come, let me fold around my heart, once more,
The sable vestments which they loved to weave.

1.—DAMES OF TROY.—*Æschylus.*

Parent of ills, the dreary air
   Diffuses sickness, terror, pain,
And dread our fatal lot to dare
   The hideous monsters of the Main.
The shaggy slopes of forests dun,
From paths of peril close the sun,
   And hide the savage prowling nigh;
Fierce vultures, signal of the storm,
Wheel round the summit's cloudy form,
   And call black tempests from the sky.

But who what dangerous schemes can tell,
   In man's aspiring bosom roll?
Or, when the tyrant passions swell,
   In woman's more impetuous soul?
If love, a burning torment, now
Shall kindle frenzy o'er the brow,
   Or fiend-like jealousy prevail?
Oh! wild the rage of woman's power,
When love and madness rule the hour,
   And gusts of baffled pride assail!

In rage the frantic Thestian gave
   The brand to burn, her son to die;

To please her foes could Scylla crave?
  Could golden bracelets steel her eye?
To please the foe, decide the strife,
She rose against her father's life,
  Stole fiend-like on his soft repose!
Approached the monarch's sacred bed,
There reft the honors of his head,
  And TRIUMPH'D with the shuddering foes!

Record the heartless deeds unsaid,
  The bloody deeds of olden time,
Enrol the loves, the guilty bed,
  Which stain this royal house of crime;
False woman's deadly hate enrol,
Against that chief of lofty soul,
  That name revered by friend and foe;
The name of Atreus fill'd the shore:
Alas! his glories blaze no more,
  A woman's hand hath laid him low.

Black annals of a distant time,
  Record in blood the Lesbian dames,
Indignant gods abhor the crime,
  And execrate the odious names;
And execrate the bloody deed
They rise; their sleeping husbands bleed,
  All slaughter'd in a single night!
Shall mortal man, with impious voice,
At deeds unhallow'd dare rejoice?
  Ye gods! ye gods! avenge the right!

Thy righteous laws, eternal king,
  Strike deep in Fate, and flourish wide;

Yea, from the rods of Justice spring;
  And scorners perish in their pride,
Portentous Fate the sword prepares
The labor of the forge she shares,
  And Fury watches for the hour!
Wide through the guilty house below
Where blood hath flow'd, fresh blood shall flow
  And Vengeance vindicate her power.

2.—OLD MEN OF SALAMIS.—*Sophocles.*

O, happy thou, illustrious Isle,
Free roving, dwelling in the sea,
To all around a joyous smile
  Still beams, fair Salamis, from thee.
But I, alas! all wretched here,
Still weeping, wasting, year by year,
  From thee allured so long ago;
Still lingering on the meadowy plain
Of distant Ida, must remain,
  While days and months uncounted flow.

Remorseless must the seasons roll,
  Revolve the night, revolve the day,
While I with worn and weary soul,
  In sorrow weep the years away?
Forever bound to cherish here
A barren hope, akin to fear,
  A hope of home and bliss again;
A fear that I shall reach before,
The dread, irremeable shore,
  The bourne of Hades' dark domain.

Infatuate with wrath divine,
  Now Ajax brings a new distress;
His woes incurable are mine—
  A waste of war, a barrenness.
Thou sent'st his conquering arm to this,
Long years ago, fair Salamis,
  And now in vain his friends condole;
His deeds of glory, welcome then,
Fall thankless now on thankless men;
  Wild frenzy now consumes his soul.

A mother somewhere soon, I know,
  Nursed by white age of ancient day,
Shall learn his soul-consuming woes;
  And not the gentle, pensive lay,
Nor yet the melancholy wail
Of piteous, plaintive nightingale,
  Ill-fated mourner, will she call;
But frantic shrieks of wild despair,
And rendings of the hoary hair,
  And blows that on the bosom fall.

Far better in the friendly grave,
  To hide from every eye secure,
Than in illusions thus to rave,
  With mockeries that must endure.
The harvest of the Grecian host,
Whose many toils the Muses boast,
  The noble son of noble sire:
His native passions all astray,
No longer keep their bright array,
  But wander, burning with a fire.

Ah! wretched sire, a dirge of woe,
   A tale of ruin waits thee here;
Soon thou, alas! must learn to know
   A weight of terror, thrill of fear.
Oh! never yet in lapse of time,
Vicissitudes of war and crime,
   Against the old Æacidæ,
Hath Envy drawn, or Hatred spun,
A blacker thread for sire and son,
   A thread of darker destiny!

3—MOTHERS OF ARGOS.—*Euripides.*

I pray thee, with these lips of age,
   I pray thee, falling at thy knee;
Thy gracious prayers I would engage,
   To free my sons from infamy.
Exposed their lifeless bodies lie,
To mountain beasts that wander by;
   Behold these piteous streams of grief;
Behold these withered hands that wreak
Vain torture on this bleeding cheek:
   Thy prayer alone may bring relief.

Thou askest why?—Ah! woe to me!
   Their bodies home I may not bear,
The mound of earth I may not see,
   Above their mouldering corses there!
O, gentle lady, much revered,
Thy bridal couch thou hast endeared,—
   A son has blessed thy Lord from thee;
Thy generous sympathy impart;
A son thou hast—a mother's heart,
   Thou may'st conceive my agony.

Implore thy son, whom we implore,
    To come to Ismenus with aid ;
His hand to mine my son's restore,
    And let the solemn rites be paid.
From dire necessity I call ;
Before these fires—thy knees, I fall :
    These mothers round your altars plead.
Our cause is holy,—be it won !
Thou art all potent in thy son,
    And Argos will revere the deed.

Companions of my gloomy way,
    Ye aged partners of my pain,
Your beaten breasts, your groans betray,
    Our speechless sorrow for the slain.
The hand of black misfortune led,
Your feet with mine, to gain the dead ;
    And gloomy Hades smiles below,
Haste, join our consecrated band ;
Oh ! tear the cheek ! Oh ! smite the hand !
    These, these the offerings of our woe.

The rock that breaks the foaming sea
    Sheds drop by droplet back again ;
Relief unspeakable to me,
    These drops of anguish for the slain.
Our noble sons have ceased to live,—
We have but sighs and tears to give,—
    These tears—our luxury of woe.
O, would each pang, each bleeding breast,
Each throbbing heart forever rest,
    Oblivions in the grave below !

4.—VERZWEIFELUNG.—*Kotzebue.*

What am I Lord! what meant to be?
  Allied to tigers, or to apes?
What aim, what plan hath God with me,
  Among these wild ferocious shapes?
Are mortal wails of anguish rung,
With feeble voice and lisping tongue,
  Sweet hallelujahs in his ear?
His offspring, writhing in his sight;
My groans, my tears his chief delight!
  Why born to sense and sorrow here?

Rush on! rush on! remorseless storm;
  These tender limbs, ye flames, consume!
Lo! what am I?—A trampled worm,
  And joyous to the skies my doom!
Come, hungry vultures of the blast;
I sink,—I spread a sweet repast,
  This quivering flesh no stinted spoil;
I moulder here, because I must,
Prepared to feast you with my dust,
  When all is o'er—my pain, my toil.

His angel did the Sire Supreme,
  His loftiest minister depute?
"Go, fly from this to that extreme,
  To each some wise endowment suit.
Behold thy younger brethren there;
A shield of life for each prepare;
  Give angels messages from me,
The lion mane, the fish its scales,
Give shells to turtles, muscles, snails,
  Down for the bird, bark for the tree."

Q

Alas! alas! celestial hate!
   He passed his youngest brother o'er!
Exposed the helpless thing to fate,
   Unclad, unkempt, defenceless, poor!
But Reason's ray he gave instead
To mock the heart, delude the head,
   And Pride to dare forbidden climes;
False hopes and fears—a restless tide,
A lust to gain, a shame to hide,
   And bitter consciousness of crime.

With bland complacency of face,
   Tray takes his bone, and sprawls along,
Nor studies rules of time and place,
   Nor dubious laws of right and wrong.
But ever conscious of his fate,
Man, man alone is doomed to wait,
   And eat his crust, prepared to die;
His dreams alarm, his doubts obscure,
But Revelation makes him sure,—
   His doom is spoken from the sky!

Am I my Maker's toy to-day,
   The dupe of pleasure, slave of pain,
Of hope the sport, of fear the prey,
   Then crumbled back to dust again?
This breathing frame, a curious shell,
In which the sounds of Ocean dwell,
   And every sound a mystery;
A thinking coil, which knows it will,
Be found a fossil on the hill,
   As years approach eternity?

O bright result of gifts divine !
   Of towering hopes, of thoughts that soar !
Pride, aspiration, aim, design,
   Of Reason, Faith, Belief of more !
This blaze—a false, delusive beam ;
This joy of life—a poet's dream,
   A meteor fading in the sea !
This Earth, with all her charms, at last,
A painted mausoleum vast,
   For panting, proud humanity !

Pride finds a mighty gulf between
   The human, and each breathing race ;
But who has truly, clearly seen
   Which hath inherited the grace ?
When first it scents the breeze's balm,
Around its mother leaps the lamb,
   Responsive to the thrill of life ;
But man must learn to walk, to eat,
To shun extremes of cold and heat,
   Precarious years of pain and strife !

Poor, crawling ape of rule and rote,
   Forever climbing for the far ;
To-day with pap in mouth and throat,
   To-morrow measuring sun and star !
Forever dreaming of the height ;
Stark blind, but conscious of a light,
   And making what he cannot find ;
He ponders, muses, overleaps
The wall that guards forbidden steeps,
   And dares Eternity behind.

Man, only man, matures to feel
　　The guilty pains of love and hate,
The flame of private, party zeal,
　　The stress and tyranny of state.
Green jealousies, and envy pale,
Low lusts, cupidities, assail,
　　And ever-during dread of death;
Hot thirst of glory, thirst of power,
Remorse that haunts the midnight hour,
　　Revenge that heats the daily breath.

With Nature's mail—tooth, talon, claw,
　　Brutes roam the hills, without appeal:
But man must guard his life, his law,
　　With arms and arsenals of steel.
He tries the softest silk display,
And jewels of the richest ray,
　　To win the long reluctant fair;
But happier creatures coo and sing,
And meet and marry every Spring,
　　Nor rank, nor gold, unites the pair.

Behold yon father, full of days;
　　Go read his latest scroll of life;
How many years in idle plays!
　　How many years in bootless strife!
One-fourth a century in sleep,
And when he waked, he waked to weep,
　　And when he smiled, he feared to smile;
For envious Fate was standing nigh,
And voices came from earth and sky,
　　The pale horse champing at the stile.

O, vanity! Of what avail,
   The beating heart the throbbing vein!
Fresh springs of hope that always fail,
   Sweet smiles that never smile again!
The morn—a breadth of feeble cries;
High noon—a blaze of burning skies,
   With disappointed dreams between;
Gray twilight brings, for coolness, care,
With fold on fold of cold despair,
   Till darkness closes sense and scene.

Our heart is wasted, day by day,
   As wishes cease, begin to burn;
We long to go, we long to stay;
   Sigh, seek to know, yet dread to learn!
Still heavier grows the load we bear,
And still the warm, obtrusive tear,
   Bedews the crust, beguiles the fast;
While Mockery leans remorseless by;
Base slander, falsehood, evil-eye
   Affright us from the world at last.

See yonder group, with lip and ear,
   And snapping lids of lambent bliss,
Intent to whisper, glad to hear
   Some fancy-speck that seems amiss.
"The deed is noble?—Say ye so?
Black spots are in the sun, ye know;
   And blind the man who fails to see;
Indeed, we must not now begin,
This traitor's registry of sin!
   His time will come! the Press is free."

And if too delicately strung,
   Some softer heart be keen to feel;
Some wretch to desperation stung,
   By sign or sigh his pang reveal,
"What can the dreamer mean?"—they say:
This ill becomes our decent day,
   This sham pretence of agony.
Despairing creature! Why complain?
We see no wrong; we feel no pain;
   Aye, 'tis the dreamer's poetry."

In yon lone hut, beside the lane,
   A stricken sire and mother lie;
Sick children cry for bread in vain;
   Affliction weeps—but no reply.
My little mite, without regret,
Before their hungry mouths I set;
   I bid the helpless eat, and live.
Oh! God! with rapture I divide;
But, hear the iron voice of pride!
   "The dreamer is too sensitive."

Aye, I must flatter, court, they say,
   And show mankind my spirit too;
"The rich," says Plato, "night and day,
   Will prosper still in all they do."
Let treason stalk from cot to tower,
Get rank, get riches, fame, and power,
   And drown the dirge of Virtue fair;
Before the Judge let Flattery stand,
With lying lip and golden hand;
   Let Justice, Mercy, Truth, despair!

Go, generous souls of golden mold,
   Go, ask them man's repute of men;
Go, learn Hypocrisy—how old?
   Inquire the birth of Slander—when?
The warm right hand you clasp to-day,
To-morrow hastens hot to slay,
   Or burns the hovel of the poor!
Oh! hide me in some deep recess;
Eve hid, for shame, her nakedness;
   Her daughters hide for shame no more!

Go, with the tooth of calumny,
   And set fraternal hearts ajar;
Teach one to rise and reap with thee
   The spoils of fratricidal war.
Ye shall be men of high renown!
For him a camp, for thee a crown
   Among the shouting sons of light;
Who pleads the right? Who stems the wrong?
Ye are triumphant, rich, and strong!
   Victorious wrong is always right!

Oh! give me back my dewy morn!
   Kind Powers, restore my natal day!
When in the grass, or blade of corn,
   The germ of my existence lay;
When I was hidden in the mead,
And felt no heart, to beat or bleed!
   Exempt from pride, exempt from pain;
Before, as milk or blood, I came
To feel a pulse, to breathe a flame,
   And kindle to a burning brain!

Didst think to ask me, POWER SUPREME,
   If I should live, and live to know,
To try, to taste the perilous beam,
   Which may be heaven or hell below?
To risk for bliss we fail to find,
The deathless tortures of a mind;
   Why call me thus to live and die?
If I MUST fall, why raise me, then,
A wretched man with wretched men,
   Far better, as I lay, to lie.

Lo! I MUST stay! compelled to stay,
   With friends and foes at every door;
Must beg for night, must beg for day,
   And swell my load of misery more!
Is it with banishment and bale,
And penal years of woe and wail,
   We buy a recompense from thee?
Oh! long this war of wrong and rue!
Redeem us, Lord; the debt is due,
   Restore our immortality!

   Frail human hearts! The MAKER will forgive.
The trampled bee will turn, and sting again;
The smitten mastiff bites the broken rod.
The rough abrasion of these rolling spheres
Meant to exalt, refine—will wring from minds
Of reverent mold, the flash of impious thought.
Affliction hath a swarming family;
And meek Humility oft starts to hear
The murmurs of her sisters—blind with grief,
And murmuring most, because the tear will blind.
This life, a mesh of misery, we lose

The uses of hard fortune, and believe
A little pain some tyranous allotment,
Harsh Edict of some unrelenting Power,
Who punishes, and feasts upon our pain ;
Who hates humanity, and loves to see
His creature writhing under Caucasus.
We fail to find the elements of things,
The causes and the reasons of our lot,
And seek Perfection where the Upas grows.
We talk of full felicities and joys,
Of bliss perennial, of the GOOD SUPREME :
Peace, nameless if a war had never been,
And Rest, that must be everlasting rest,
Nor deem such Rest eternal misery.
And yet, we know each drop of bliss, the sum
Of countless drops filtrated from the Flood,
And rounded by the winds that terrify ;
A ripple in the summer sea of life,
Which would be tempest in a wintry night.
The shade, so grateful when the sun is high,
Some chilly day, may bring the death we dread.
I know not what is Evil, what is Good,
Or sickness what, or pain, or pleasing sense,
Or what uncounted sympathies attune
My soul to Nature's harmonies to-day,
Or why I feel some jarring in the chords.
Yet music needs a discord, now and then ;
All these, I hold, are elements of Good ;
How else would dust have tasted joy at all ?

 To sharpen, means to grind. Activities
Which smooth and harmonize discordant forms,
Are quarried from the granite hills around ;

And whirling grooves, with rude asperities,
Pour the white flour of life for hungry mouths.
Silk is too soft for happiness. The garb
Of coarsest woof protects us in the blast.
I suffer life's inclemencies, and prove
To heart and soul, the elements I need.
In very truth, the penalty of pain
Begets the consolation, which is sweet.
Am I not proud to find a triumph here,
A CONSOLATION, angels may not know?
O, mortal! trust me, all is right and true.
A friendly hand revolves the wheels of Fate.
These elements of Destiny secure,
Will bear me yonder, in the lapse of years,
Where bloom emerges from the seeds of pain.

GOOD AND EVIL.

Idyl III.—Voices of "Hilltop."

Amore alma e del monde, Amore e mente.

MAY.

Sweet May and I came down the vale,
   By the home we loved in days of yore,
Her balmy breath had sweetened the gale,
   And the banks were rich with rosy store.
The linnet, the lark, and oriel
Were chanting the loves they chant so well;
It was blue all above, below all green,
With the radiant glow of noon between;
And ever the corner and crossing way
Advised us to listen what Truth would say;
For her winsome smile kept luring along,
Discussing with Life the right and the wrong.
Now wider and warmer the prospect grew,
Massanutten unbound his mail of blue,
Green ridges of oak, in sunlight arrayed,
Cast hollow and dale in a deeper shade,
And runnel and rill, with leap of delight,
From dingle and dell came flashing in sight,
And winding his way, like Glory, below,
In glancing curves came the old Shenandoah.

Void of intelligence, void of a will,
The forces of Nature their mission fulfill,
But man, in his prowess, his passion, his pride,
Aspires,—and the beautiful cannot abide.
Lo, yonder the foot of the spoiler hath trod!
A curse overshadows the blessings of God!
Sweet coverts of Eden now darkened with dust,
With cinder the flume, the railway with rust!
Dim paths over fields uncultured entwine,
The croft and the holt no limits define,
The meadow, the orchard, the garden, the glade,
Confess no distinction but sunshine and shade!
Lo, yonder, the town, but a century grown,
Now proffers a darken'd, a desolate zone!
Lone chimneys uncoif'd look solemnly down
On ashes, and ruins, and rocks with a frown!
Oh! madness of folly! Oh! frenzy of hate!
Is this to be glorious, this to be great?
Do anguish and tears, do havoc and flame,
Fit mortals for freedom, fit spirits for fame?
Friends of Beauty and Truth! explain, sweet May!
Friend of plenty and peaceful prosperity, say,
Friend of roses and rainbows! tell if you can.
What mystery is this in the spirit of man?

"Ceres has gone with Diana for seed:
Our FIELDS have become independent indeed;
Purlieus and impalings, in bounds that inclose,
They feel to be cruel restraints I suppose.
Now, I love enclosures, things that confine
My rose of the garden from wild eglantine.
Hence, war is a terror, a tyrant to me;
Politicians and reason could never agree:

They say I am foolish, and timid, and tame ;
Hence, Hate gets the glory, and Love all the blame !
  "The Right and the Just by force to defend,
To shield from defilement thy household, thy friend,
When Innocence suffers, the battle to breast,
Is reason's, humanity's, nature's behest ;
Unsheathe every sword, if Liberty bleed, —
The voice of necessity hallows the deed ;
Let Justice, not Glory, give vengeance her brand,
And patriots may legions of angels command.
I urge not a faction, — I speak to the race ;
All warfare's devoid of glory and grace.
Fate molded in man a deep sense and strong,
Of Right to do right, of Wrong to do wrong ;
The mandate of Conscience is radiant with light,
"Assail not the Right ! Assail not the Right."

  " Ask you, what is glory ? Behold yonder spire !
There monthly the guardians of justice retire ;
There issue decrees, — the best for the best ;
How none shall be injured, none shall molest ;
How purity, plenty, and peace shall abound,
Till Shenandoah glistens with Edens around.
Ask you, what is glory ? Look here, look there ;
A hundred sweet faces smile out on the air.
The light of my countenance loves to repose
Among those dear dimples that rival the rose.
I tell thee, no spot in the Valley can show
More musical mold, more guiltless a glow.
Their manners how sweet, how gentle, how true !
Their kindness as genial and soft as the dew :
The smile of their innocence, like the mild ray,
That links the first star with a calm closing day.

Ask you, what is glory?—List to that strain,
Which peals with an echo that echoes again,—
The spirit of melody, ling'ring to tell
How blissful the bosoms around us that swell.
In life's Melodrama each place acts a part,
In toil or amusement, in science or art,—
Some noted for piety, some for their sins,
Some skilled to make perfumes, some to make pins;
Here Beauty and Music agree to preside,
Where virtue is glory, and honor is pride."

Sweet May, I believe thee. From fountain and air,
Emerges the lovely, unbosoms the fair;
The romance of scene, inspiration of place,
Gives beauty a witchery, glances a grace.
The glory of Greece was her mind and her mold,
The soft of Ionia, of Doris the bold,
But something of loftier, nobler line,
Gives Beauty and Music a pathos divine;
Something that smiles from the fountains above,
And named by the sweet liquid syllable,—Love.
Love came in the bosom of Truth from Heaven,
When man to Promethean fetters was given.
O, Love is the charm interwoven with all
The tones that enchant us, the smiles that enthrall!
Love brings down to earth the dews and the showers,
Love rules o'er the roses, the birds, and the bowers,
The touching of hands, and the meeting of lips,
The nectar the bee and the butterfly sips.
Love mounts to the sky, and extends her control,
From planet to sun, from needle to pole;
For fate has decreed, philosopher's tell,
Some atoms to marry, and some to repel,

This physical law works its sequel in mind,
Repulsions, affinities, bind and unbind.

Lo, yonder the gallery of Barnet invites ;
Ascend, bonny May, emulation excites.
You paint the rose-buds, and Barnet paints you ;
His pencil, Aureola stealing a view.
Light golden Ariels friendly and fleet,
Kissing all faces most lovely and sweet,
Bearing all beautiful bosoms and heads,
Away in a rapture to Iodine beds.
And here comes a Naiad, all living in smiles ;
I strive to recall her, but mem'ry beguiles :—
O, yes, it is Sallie, the bride of the bard,
Bright as the sunbeam giving green to the sward ;
Bride of the bard whom the Muses name TAU,
Who sang Opakanka, that Legend of awe ;
Whose soul, in the mirror of soul, can discern,
Heaven makes the IDEAL the TRUE that we learn.
To him was entrusted a Lyre at his birth,
And many wild strains he has caught for the earth ;
And more, many more, let us trust, he will bring,
For Culture to study, for Beauty to sing.

JUNE.

Beneath the moon, the orient moon,
   Fair empress of the sky,
The flowery fields and hills of June,
   The lovely meadows lie ;
And gleaming now, now briefly hid
On yonder hill, you bower amid,
   A star-like taper burns.
Each night I gaze, in joy and tears,—
The bliss of long remember'd years,
   In streams of light returns ;
For heaven had linked my brightest day
In radiance with that home of Gray.

And Beauty now,—a charming band,
   Adorns you mansion high ;
The thrilling touch of tender hand,
   The light of smiling eye ;
There beings bright, and pure, and fair,
Breathe incense on the fragrant air,
   Shed lustre on the light.
For chill the summer breezes stray,
Pale, cheerless, cold, the Summer day,
   And dim the starry night,
If Beauty, Purity, and Love,
Shine not within, around, above.

They say, when Evening shuts the rose,
   And cools the sultry air,
The setting Sun enamor'd throws
   Celestial splendors there.

Aye,—well may fond Hyperion's ray,
Delight to linger and delay,
  On window, door, and hall,
He deems his Euryphissa there,
Hope brightens so his golden hair.
  You almost hear him call;
And gazing from the dappled West.
He looks his last, intensest, best.

Blest lot of humble life to meet,
  In hospitable hall,
The young, the innocent, the sweet,
  The gray-haired sire and all;
To scan the portraits Orra drew,
Familiar features, strong and true,
  Sage Webster, good and great;
Blithe Sallie's queries try between,
The apple and the Cyprian queen,
  Sad source of Priam's fate;
For lately from Carara's mine,
Visini carved that form divine.

The moon has climbed her starry dome,
  That taper gleams no more:
Delicious visions wait me home.
  Delicious dreams of yore.
Old waves of thought voluptuous swell
And rainbows spread amid the spell.
  Arcades of love and light.
Oh! what were slumber's drowsy kiss,
To golden visions such as this,
  Through all the wakeful night?

Sweet voices throng the dulcet air,
And whisper moonlight music there!

Chorus of Voices.—*On the Lawn.*

Arborets of crystal stone,
Gems and spars in caverns lone,
Coralline impearled with dew,
Coves with runlets breaking through;
Waving pines upon the glade
Lilies peeping from the shade;
Gentle airs that whisper sweet
Silver brooks that murmuring meet,
Choral birds amid the thorn,
Hymning symphonies of morn;
Winding herds along the lane,
Lambkins sporting on the plain,
Laughing maidens in the mead,
Swains that follow, swains that lead,
Sight, and sound, and solace, these
Heaven hath left below, to please,
Soft, refined, inspiring, gay
Emblems true of thee and May,
      Lovely Orra Gray.

Semichorus.—*In the Grove.*

Stars that shine in silence high
Aerolites that skim the sky,
Cloudlets tipp'd with rosy ray
Sent from Pleiads far away;
Murmurs that you scarce can hear,
Stealing softly, sweet, and near;

Shadowy forms you scarce can see,
Gliding down the moonlit lea ;
Wandering winds that kiss your cheek,
Pausing there, as if to speak ;
Voices, hovering in the air,
Kindling hope, dispelling care ;
Harps unseen from arbors pealing,
Tales of youth and love revealing ;
Nature's types of modesty,
Images of June and thee,
Pure as Lyra's dewy ray,
Gentle as a shepherd's lay,
      Gentle Sallie Gray!"

If in these hearts, so kind and pure,
One thought of better days endure,
That thought, a star of fadeless ray,
Would light me down a devious way ;
And Memory cling a living joy!
Sou VIENDRIEZ-VOUS DE MOI!

ORRA.

The clouds retire, the storm is o'er,
The vivid lightning darts no more,
'Twas awful but sublime to see,
How fierce it smote yon aged tree!
There came a lull—a mute repose,
No droplet fell—no murmur rose ;
A moment, and the towering oak
Convulsive crash'd in flame and smoke ;
But now dissolved the black array,
The harmless lightnings sport and play.

To flowery meads the frugal bee,
Renews his wanderings, glad and free.
No more of sultry heats afraid,
The browsing herds forsake the shade;
And youths and maids, with laughing eye,
Again in noisy tumult hie.
For now afar from Indian Isles,
The sun returns his parting smiles.

 From yonder height diverging streams,
The pencil of his rosy beams,
Which swells or narrows, as the breeze,
In fitful dalliance waves the trees,
On yonder summit far away,
The dropping clouds imbibe his ray,
And bend the many-colored bow,
High o'er the glittering hills below.
The trees, that crown the summit bright,
Wave proudly in the golden light,
And sun and shower their charms employ,
To make this world, a world of joy.

DALNI.

But I, alas! no joy derive,
 From all you see around;
In vain for me the seasons strive
 To robe the teeming ground,
For darkness long hath clothed my soul,
And shades eternal o'er me roll.
No more for me the beams of morn,
With rosy hue the hills adorn;
For me no more the stars unite
Their lustre on the brow of Night,

The fresher breeze, the warmer ray,
Is all I know of night or day.

   The flowers embalmed in early dews,
Their scents alone for me diffuse;
In vain their rival colors vie,
To woo aside the rayless eye;
One settled cloud of stubborn gloom
Conceals their beauty and their bloom.
And when at evening I am led,
Through still unyielding gloom, to bed,
How oft in half-distracted mood,
These melancholy thoughts obtrude:
Oh! that when morn's renascent beams,
Enrobe the vales and gild the streams;
When half the world awakes to view,
I could arise, and see it too!
But ah! there shines no morn for me,
No dewy lawn, no waving tree;
Embosomed in a living tomb,
A cold, intense, unyielding gloom;
I hear a thousand voices sound,
Like spirits murmuring under ground.
My struggling soul attempts to fly,
From shore to shore, from earth to sky;
Amass new stores of light divine,
Dispose, compare them, and combine;
For light to me is like the smile
Of one who charmed our youth awhile,
And ere we thought the joy could die,
The smile, the charm forever fly;
Yet in the soul a lingering light
Shines like a lonely star at night

Though pale and dim the faded ray,
It cannot vanish all away.

ORRA.

My pensive Dalni, if the mind
Can aught in cold description find,
Which may a hopeless loss beguile,
And give thy shaded brow a smile,
Both morn and eve I will assay
To calm, or chase that shade away;
Yes, at the noon of night arise,
And read for thee the starry skies;
Each faded scene, thy memory's store,
To all its former charms restore;
Its beauty and its bloom repair,
And keep it ever smiling there.

Now, far behind yon breezy height,
The sun withdraws his temper'd light,
No more his long, unbending beams,
In glittering lines o'erarch the streams
And lifted by the swelling shade,
Aloft the fleecy clouds pervade;
For still around departing day,
The fragments of the storm delay,
High flush'd with glowing splendor o'er,
They spurn the clouds that rain no more;
Some stoop to drink the rosy beam,
Like red leaves floating on the stream,
Of lighter form, and paler hue,
Some rise, and vanish from the view.

DALNI.

Ah, cease! nor strive to make me sigh,
That stars are e'en more blest than I.
If each bright orb you now review,
In light and joy its path pursue;
If still eternal light divine,
Delights all conscious eyes but mine,
And worlds around, and suns above,
Rejoice in beauty, light, and love;
If e'en the fleecy clouds of even,
Delighted drink the beams of heaven,
And dance and revel in the ray,
That woo'd them from the dewy spray,
The blooming flower, the leafy tree;
The dust I feel, but cannot see,
And loathsome worms that basking lie,
Are more beloved of heaven than I!
To me the banquets of the mind
Are luxuries, are joys, refined;
I loved in early youth to climb
At night some breezy height sublime,
To watch the stars, till rosy dawn
Brought forth the roe and nimble fawn;
Then o'er the rocks and ledges hie,
To view them as they wandered by:
Or on the bank recline to read
Of glorious death, or noble deed.

ORRA.

Repress thy murmurs. Does the shower,
In vain for thee refresh the bower,
And call the balmy breeze to blow,
Diffusing fragrance all below.

Do yonder hills in vain resound,
A thousand melodies around?
Does Art, with emulative strain,
In mellow murmurs walk the plain?
If gelid winds unfeeling blow,
And freeze the lucid streams below,
Say, does the sun in vain arise,
To warm the air, and clear the skies?
When Autumn pours his fruits around,
And luscious plenty loads the ground,
Canst thou not, too, enjoy the store,
From Nature's bounty flowing o'er?
For thee on far Arabian hills,
The incense breathes, the myrrh distils;
The minstrel leaves a foreign shore,
And pours for thee his treasured lore;
Iberian shepherds shear their flocks,
The Russian flays his mailed ox;
For thee adventurous sails convey,
The grateful tea from far Cathay;
Rich India rears the juicy cane;
Brown olives strew the Italian plain,
Then seize the joys that still remain,
And scorn to pine at partial pain.

GOOD AND EVIL.

Idyl IV.—Waif of Rosendale.

CANTO I.—ROSENHALL.

"Fleet on the tempest blown,
 Far from the mountain dell,
Rose in their cloudy cone,
 Elfin and Spell;
Woo'd by the spirit tone,
 Trembling and chill,
Wandered a maiden lone,
 On the bleak hill :
  Mau-in-waun-du-me-nung,
   Trembling and chill.

"Low in the moory dale,
 Green mossy waters flow,
Under the drowsy gale,
 Moaning and slow ;
There in her snowy veil,
 Bleeding and bound,
Lay the sweet damsel pale,
 On the cold ground,
  Mau-in-waun-du-me-nung,
   On the cold ground.

T

"Sad o'er her sunken head,
  Waved the low linden spray ;
Wither'd leaves, sear and red,
  Fell where she lay,
Cold on her icy bed,
  Silent and lorn
Lies the lost maiden dead!
  Why was she born?
    Mau-in-waun-du-me-nung,
  Why was she born?

"Now, tell me, regent of the Dale,
What dove divine, or nightingale,
Thus stirs with her melodious pain,
The echoes of the hill and plain?
That tone is more than earthly tone :
A rapture mingled with a moan,
So modulates this genial air,
We feel an angel must be there.
I knew not if in sigh or sound,
Could dwell emotions so profound :
I knew not if this air could be
Symphonious with Immensity :
And soul and sense be borne away
Beyond the bounds of solar day.
No syllable of human speech,
Could thus the depths of Being reach ;
It seem'd the trembling, waving tone
Came from a world I once had known,
And thrills of feeling, streams of thought,
Embosomed in the deep, were wrought,
And gave melodious waves to flow
Far down the years of long ago."

Thus spoke a stranger, passing by ;
The master of the hall and I,
Enchanted, by the fence reclin'd ;
The waters murmur'd close behind,
The smooth and verdant slope, before,
Rose gently to the mansion door,
And we were dreaming o'er the scene,
So sweetly molded, so serene.
It is a green and smiling swell,
A spot for happiness to dwell ;
It seems that Nature shapes a plan,
And molds a dwelling spot for man,
And this was meant to be the home
Of loves and joys that never roam.

Then came the cheerful, quick reply :
"My daughters love that voice, and I,
Our little waif, Elaine, is there ;
She often sings that tender air.
We took her, when deserted found,
An infant weeping on the ground.
Her mother, sire, no mortal knows,
Except the pastor of Melrose ;
And he evades, declines to tell,
Some truth, I fear he knows too well.
I see him often passing by ;
He scans these grounds with curious eye ;
Whate'er he may have known, or knows,
He seems to watch her as she grows ;
They brought her here, a very child,
Feeble but patient, silent, mild.
We love her, as we love our own ;
She is so sweet in word and tone,

She never wept. All day and night
A smile lives in those eyes of light;
Each day and night, she seems to grow
More lovely as the seasons go.
So soft, and beautiful, and sweet,
We feel like falling at her feet,
Like worshiping the angel mild,
That grew and grows within the child.

"She heard my ruder workmen swear!
She trembl'd, shudder'd, ran with fear,
And told us that the men would die;
She saw their Maker passing by,
And in his hand there was a spear,
And in his eye there was a tear.
My daughters sometimes disagree;
We are not overwise, you see;
But sweet Elaine will run to each,
With soothing word, amusing speech,
And soon the laughter of the soul
Breaks out, and all their hearts are whole.
Sometimes a keen reproof, or hiss,
Will chide her if too free, remiss;
She pauses, bows in silent thought,
And on her smooth, white brow is wrought
A soul communing with a soul,
The light and love of Self-control.

"I would not tax your patient ear;
But I might tell things strange to hear,
Now at the verge of womanhood,
So gentle, docile, kind, and good,
She has accomplishments so rare,
And how secured, or when, or where,

Is still a mystery to all,
Who live, admire, in Rosenhall
Her, schools, her teachers have been few ;
She knows at once what others knew,
Her teacher comes, and leaves his soul,
Elaine obtains, enjoys the whole,
She talks sometimes in tongues unknown,
And laughs at words she hears alone ;
While o'er her brow a joyous glow,
Seems from the silent void to flow ;
And then it were a bliss to see
The beauty of this mystery,
The lustre of those eyes that view
The vacancy, for me and you.

"If those who love us come to see,
She seems all joyous, friendly, free ;
Mysterious instinct seems to tell
What feelings in each bosom dwell,
She melts in joy the Summer day,
She cheats the winter nights away ;
Before you think the dawn is here,
Still reverent the listening ear,
Some fragrant flower she finds for each,
Some lovely smile, enchanting speech,
She takes the lute, attunes the string ;
The young, the old prepare to sing,
But should an envious foe obtrude,
She darts away in solitude.

"That holy man, who lives, they say,
Beyond this mountain, came one day,
A man of winning, warm address,
A something words will not express ;

Large, molded well, commanding eye;
But leering as you pass him by.
With pious, condescending air,
He stops to ask you how you fare,
And would assist you, if you need;
But then you are his slave indeed.
Melrose and Mundleville declare
His eloquence beyond compare,
And thousands flock to hear him tell,
The fiery pains of sin and hell.
He came one day;—our little waif,
Affrighted sought an iron safe,
And hid her there, the timid child!
How could she be so rude and wild?
At first he call'd with soothing tone:
She nestled there all night alone;
Nor could we hear her breathing more,
Nor move the safe, nor move the door:
Next day all day he stay'd to see,
The little timid mystery,
He begg'd, entreated, threaten'd, swore:
No voice, no stir within that door.
That night he left; we breathed again,
The safe released our dear Elaine,
But all she knew, or would declare,—
"Dear mother call'd and kept me there!"

"Since older, wiser, now she tells,
Of wondrous powers and potent spells,
And says we cannot see nor hear
The influence of sphere on sphere,
The beauteous angels, cloth'd in light,
That come and go, both day and night,

Bright spirits of the earth and air,
That from the deep Unseen repair,
That shield from ill, or wipe the tear,
Or pass on pinions softly near.
"Oh! if"—she says, "We all could see
This busy, friendly pageantry,
This cavalcade of living forms,
Amid the tempests and the storms,
This world would be a blest abode,
And life a smoother, safer road."

"Once, and but once, a year ago,
 When all the week was drear and rainy,
Calling on Jake, and now on Joe,
 To read the monthly miscellany.
When with a shock, we missed Elaine.
Amid the beating of the rain,
We call'd, we called; she answer'd not;
We search'd the safe, the Hall, the cot;
The barn, the grove; the neighbors came.
The young, the old with trembling frame;
For all that knew her; loved her well,
The hand that touch'd you bore a spell,
Erasmus raving frantic o'er
The building, reach'd the garret floor,
And there, within an angle, lay,
The darling all that rainy day,
We brought her to her chamber bed
Alas! She breath'd not:—Was she dead?
Her pulse had ceased, and yet the hue,
No signs of death betray'd to view,
Three days we stood in terror there,
We watched her lips, her bosom fair,

We tried each little art we knew,
Until the deadly shade withdrew;
At last she sigh'd, and smiling rose.
What now she tells, what now she knows,
Is wondrous, lofty, recondite,
Too far above our feeble light."

CANTO II.—THE SNARE.

"My herd was breaking for the shade:
They ran, they drew me up the glade;
No time to loiter, or to roam;
I wished to turn and take them home.
Behind the hills the day had gone,
And shadows deepen'd on the lawn;
A voice that sounded like a knell,—
A fearful voice, I knew too well,
Sarcastic, smote me like a blow;
I ceased to turn; I ceased to go,
Out leap'd a voice behind a pine,
"I have you now! you must be mine."
That instant came a human hand,
And clasp'd me like an iron band.
"You, lovely sylph! you must be mine!"
He said between a snarl and whine.
I know not if the Lord was there;
I heard dear mother, in the air,
"Fly, fly, Lorraine! from ruin fly!"
The rude hand trembled,—so did I.

But leaping with disdain away,
I flew; he follow'd, bent to slay!
O'er rock, o'er ravine, forest, fell,
Up rugged hill, down dreary dell,
The huge, dark woods confin'd the view,
I knew not what I did, should do;
For near, still near, his pantings sped;
That iron hand was at my head;
I leaped the ravines, fallen trees;
I climb'd the rocks on hands and knees;
I turned, returned, I knew not how;
The fiend implored, entreated now;
For just before me open'd wide,
A field upon the water side;
I saw, I sought this cottage door;
I knew no more; I know no more."

Thus spoke Elaine, as passed away
The tumult of her first dismay,
When, waking from her swoon, she found
No matron, maidens gather'd round.
I softly soothed her modesty;
Erasmus left it all to me,
And now, with silent step withdrew,
Now came, and leaned, and listen'd too.
Now ran with anxious haste to bring
A cool libation from the spring:
And bathed her lily temples oft,
And touch'd her brow, so mild, so soft.
He stripp'd our rose-bush bare, I know,
Such fragrance seem'd around to flow;
We had a rare, delicious grape
So large, alluring, hue and shape,

He durst not reach the dainty prize ;
His look the needful hint supplies ;
And if I should have proffer'd all,
Our riches ha l outshone the Hall.
Indeed, the damsel seem'd to see,
Her thanks not always due to me.

But when her fearful tale was told,
He felt not young, nor I felt old.
Ah! had you seen our eyes that night,
We both were warriors, men of might.
And if that man, what though he be
Of Samson mold, or potency,
Had just been there that blessed hour,
To learn, to feel, that Love is power,
Next sacred morn, the rising sun
Had hail'd a deed of justice done.
Oh! sad that science may not know,
Just where and when should fall the blow.
Just where and when, triumphant Wrong
Is proudly weak, and meanly strong!
Poor Sympathy, too slow to learn,
She weeps, but wets the Sufferer's urn.
She could have saved your darling slain,
But now she wails your wailings vain,
She could have fill'd a home with joy,
But now she weeps your famished boy.

And yet we hold a sacred trust,
  We know sweet Sympathy supernal,
This fellowship of dust with dust,
  This consciousness of life eternal:
I cannot see you suffer now ;
I chase the wrinkles from your brow,

Because I feel that you and I
Need something holier than to die.
And then I love you, if I see,
My presence your felicity.
And you requite me, if I stay,
Your Love, which is eternal pay.

Thus suffering passes into bliss,
And Love declines his world for this,
You oft have seen the fair, the fond;—
A glance presume, a blush respond;
The look, the smile, the sigh convey
The inward soul to outward day;
But had you seen two beings now,
And read the scroll of cheek and brow;
Had seen them look and lean so near,
The smile communing with the tear,
You would have felt and ponder'd well
The Beauty I can never tell,
  Through images disclosing;
That pain may have its mission too,
And fear and terror much to do,
  To make the hint imposing.
A snowy breast lay half revealed,
Beneath the lips that would have sealed,
  Immortal rapture there;
The gentle sigh, the lips apart,
The heaving of a human heart,
  Unwritten hopes declare.
No Paris on his dewy bed
Of hyacinths and roses red,
  Had dreams so near divine;
A beam embodied in a bower,

Where every plant contains a flower,
Faint Light, Elaine, to thine!

 Quick o'er her heaving breast she drew
A silken vest of purple hue,
And rose to seek her home again,
But how? The night had gather'd rain:
"I bless benignant fate that drew
My feet to safety, and to you;
I trust some friendly hand will guide
My steps; you know where we reside.
This is the only boon I crave,
And less would ill become the brave."
The tone so sweet, reproof so kind,
At least restored an absent mind.
Erasmus felt, too warm a friend,
If o'er-officious, might offend.
"Genius, or angel, if thou be!
Forgive a look too bold or free!"
But words were cold for what he felt;
He falter'd, and before her knelt.
"If I too bold, thro' love of bliss
A bliss, too sweet for world like this;
Too fondly cast a thoughtless eye,
Too deeply drank one fragrant sigh,
May not contrition reinstall?
Devotion was the cause of all.
This hut is poor; its tenants lone,
No more we hear a mother's tone;
She left her smile, she left a tear,
To live within our bosoms here.
But here repose, and dread no ill;
The night is dark, the air is chill,

Ah! palsied may the bosom be,
Which holds one thought to injure thee!
At dawn the rain may cease to fall,
Thou shalt re-enter Rosenhall.
Or I will go, with rapid feet,
And find conveyance warm and meet."
Again her heart, with sudden glow,
Beat hard, and heaved her breast of snow,
And oft her eyes with dewy ray,
The tumult of her soul betray,
And once the words, in whisper, fell,
"This is my angel's Arrionel!"

Sharp from without, impetuous came
A shout, a call, a yell, a name;
Amid the darkness and the rain,
The mountains echoed back, "Elaine!"
A rush of tumult shakes the ground,
The woods with various cries resound;
The rifle's peal, the neigh of steed!
The rustling boughs, the crashing reed;
The horsemen darting from the height,
Break out of darkness into sight,
And footmen, threading the ravine,
Emerge and peer around the scene.

We rush without, and call aloud;
The sound arrests the scatter'd crowd;
From hill and dell the hunters pour;
They throng the yard, surround the door,
And now loud peals of glad relief,
Proclaim the end of fear and grief.
O, proud result of long suspense!
First thanks to gracious Providence,

And thanks to us, and tears of joy,
And grasping hands with man and boy.
And busy tongues and questions rife,
A rush of renovated life.
All burned to know, yet none could wait,
Too slow the tongue that may relate.
How blest to find yourself the prize,
The jewel of admiring eyes!
When all you honor, all you know,
Rejoice to meet you still below!
Dear image of that richer love,
With which the holy meet above.
O, happiest lot of life to see
My presence your felicity,
And happiest too to leave mankind
A legacy of love behind;
A fragrance in the memory,
A tone of lasting melody,
At last was heard the maiden's tale;
Some faces black, and some were pale,
The priest salacious had his due;
For he it was, the youngest knew;
Her faithful portrait showed the man;
Some guessed the object, some the plan,
For long, had private whispers run,
His schemes, his aims, his mischiefs done:
And all averred, if seen again,
The prowling preacher might be slain.

 In Rosenhall the lights are shining;
  The lost, the loved at home again,
 The master on his couch reclining,
  Must hear the song of dear Elaine,

"Invite, invite our friends to-morrow,
A feast must be surcease of sorrow;
A day of mirth and music waits,
With open doors, and open gates."

CANTO III.—SUSPENSE.

1. "I'll weave a wreath of bright hues three,
   For the brow of my charming youth,
And say, You must wear it, my love, for me,
   This garland of love and truth.
For as its beauty and perfume,
   Are shed for thee alone,
Thy true Lorraine, and her youthful bloom,
   While they last, shall be thine own.
      My love:
While they last, shall be thine own.

2. "But as its sweets, so fragrant now,
   Must soon be sigh'd away,
Its leaves upon thy happy brow,
   Soon wither and decay,
These charms you love must wither too,
   This heart lie cold and lone;
But thou wilt know, Oh! deep and true,
   They once were all thine own,
      My love;
They once were all thine own.

3. "Not I to Roman, golden shrine,
   My orisons can pay;
Thy God, thy worship shall be mine,
   Through loving night and day;
When thou shalt seek, at dewy morn,
   Some holy spot alone,
Lorraine shall still thy side adorn,
   Thy prayer shall be her own,
      My love;
   Thy prayer shall be her own.

4. "I knew a prayer, dear mother taught
   My infant lips to say;—
Sweet words my dawning memory caught,
   Are warm and fresh to-day:—
And when she pass'd, I pray'd it o'er,
   Aye, oft in tears alone,
This prayer and thine are two no more;
   They both are all your own,
      My love;
   They both are all your own.

5. "I'll be an Houri, fond and fair,
   In Tooba grove with you,
A Peri of the lucid air,
   Less beautiful than true.
And when you muse, or wish, or sigh,
   Will bring this fragrant zone,
A faithful bliss, forever nigh,
   A life which is your own,
      My love;
   A life which is your own."

GOOD AND EVIL.

Within the orchard sang the maid:
Her voice re-echoed from the shade,
So clear and full, so near the Hall,
She seem'd within her room to all.
A week before, a festive throng
Had traced these pleasant shades along;
A week before, though grieved to yield,
She ceased to drive her kine afield,
And tempted not the road or lane,
The bowers, the winding lawns again,
She shunned the banks, she trod no more
The pleasant walks, so loved before.
Admirers came and passed away
The lonely night, the golden day,
And happiness was in the Hall,
Security the trust of all.
Erasmus came and talked of Fate,
And Providence, and Life, and Hate,
And what he thought mankind should do.
To make this world an Eden too;
But never told his dear Elaine,
That Life is Love, and Love is Pain.

That melody resounds no more,
On casement, hall, and corridor;
Shall never in these hills again,
Resound the voice of sweet Elaine?
Alarm has spread,—a strange sensation,
 Came with that sudden, faint refrain.
A quick distress of suffocation,
 A sense of danger and Elaine.
Her chamber first, the house, the hall
They penetrate—they fly, they call:

The alleys, bowery walks, the lawn,
They probe, they pierce, from dark to dawn.
In vain, in vain! the fields, the cot;
They range, explore, but find her not.
The pride and beauty of the hall,
Sons, daughters, mother, sire and all,
Are out among the hills again,
For days they search, but search in vain,
Out-worn and weary in their sorrow,
Return to wait and search to-morrow.
The kine, expectant at the gate,
Delay at eve, and look, and wait;
More lonely seem the mountains now:
The leaves are fading on the bough;
The mountain rose and eglantine,
Withhold their fragrance, and decline.
The flowers rejoice to see us live;
Their smiles, their grateful fragrance give;
But now the dearest life withdrawn
That ever graced this flowery lawn,
   Hath left them all repining;
They will not bloom, they cannot grow,
In all this rush of human woe,
   Our fondest hopes declining.

And Hope, we know, sweet Hope will stay,
If all our friends have passed away,
When Reason dies upon his throne,
Illusive hope will still atone,
The wintry steeps of age along,
Still whisper her consoling song,
And e'en at Evil's latest lair,
We find that death is not despair.

'Tis life's unbounded telescope,—
This brave tenacity of hope !
It sees the love at last descend,
The Good begin, the Evil end,
I bless the hopes that still believe ;
I know that heaven will not deceive.

The circles of their search profound,
Embrace the distant hills around ;
Embrace the day, the starry night,
For stars did not refuse their light ;
Yet stars had seen, but would not tell,
What bearing might dissolve the spell.
Suspense ! suspense ! and did she live ?
Nine days !—Ha ! Reason hope to give ?
Oh ! was her life on earth no more,
We might inter ; we might deplore.
If dead, it were relief to know ;
Suspense, the worst of ills below.
And now, at night, within the Hall,
Friends, neighbors sat in silence all ;
Some new suggestions, half afraid,
Half-utter'd, whisper'd in the shade.
And thus in council dim, they lay
The labors for another day.
But who would touch harmonious string,
And where the voice would dare to sing ?
The young, the beautiful were there,
But on each brow a gloomy care ;
And music, Siren of the soul,
Had turned to poison in the bowl.
Ah ! what is pleasure ! what is pain !
You ask the lute, the lyre in vain.

Is Ill a thing we frame or find,
An outward fact, or mood of mind ?
What is the pleasure, when I hear
The sounds that transport, ravish, cheer !
What is the pain ? these tones will now
Transfix with anguish breast and brow !
   The circles widen. Far the woe
Impels them on and on to go :
They pass the hills, the mountain blue,
And Mundleville is startled too ;
The Parsonage is probed in vain,
The Parson smiles, but no Elaine !
He smiles—that unctuous, wily brow,
Had learned to smile; had practiced how.
This pious priapism of face,
Some hold a supernatural grace ;
It is a winning, wondrous string,
A smooth, regenerative thing,
Which draws the muscles as you please,
Much art will manage it with ease ;
But if your skill be not mature,
A flash of truth is insecure.
I know not if the Parson was adept,
Long years he had one guilty secret kept,
Another now had multiplied his toil,
It might demand a new supply of oil,
But now, he smiles with that contemptuous smile,
Which squeezes through the lambent lids of guile.

   Erasmus read him o'er and o'er,
Conjoined the seen, the hints before ;
The lines which struggling Nature drew,
In feature, lineament, and hue :

The red, the pale, restrained, revealed,
The guilt betray'd, the guilt concealed.
No terror there; but wrath restrain'd,
A triumph veiled, a sadness feign'd,
Deep in the soul, a truth was plain;
He had traduced the dear Elaine;
But where was she? and where the proof?
The web is darker than the woof;
Each cranny, corner, nook, defile,
Is tortured, tested, mile by mile.
In vain! in vain!—heart-broken now,
Erasmus pressed his throbbing brow;
He had, beneath the fatal blow,
Thought more of action than of woe;
But now a paleness crept apace,
O'er lips and temples, brow and face;
The bloom forsook his youthful years,
And o'er the frozen fount of tears,
  A wintry frost had driven,
The glossy lustre left his hair,
A sudden snow from Boreal air,
  The hues of Age had given.

"Elaine, dear mystery of my heart," he said;
"Thou Æon of the Summer Isles ahead,
If that sweet soul, so luminous, so pure,
Hath gone from earth, and left us to endure;
It would be easy, and my heart could find,
Where we might meet, immortal mind with mind.
But who will tell? Thou mayst be mured alone,
In some dark cave, or charnel vault unknown.
If so, the duty of my life must be,
To search, to find, to set my darling free.

I deem not how to turn, or where to go;
Deep mysteries of life beset me so!
Ye mountain dales, I thread you back again;
I know, I know, ye saw my lost Elaine;
This air she breathed, not many days ago,
This evening beam was on that brow, I know;
These rocks and trees, this drooping mountain grass,
They saw her too; I know they saw her pass;
Sun, mountain, air, why give ye not report?
How can ye make a broken heart your sport?
Ye saw her dragged by ruffian hands away,
And yet ye keep it hidden, night and day.
I know ye loved her, know ye grieved to see
The sacrilege that ruin'd her and me.

   Ye know this arm would rescue if I knew,
Ye know concealment is to be untrue,
And yet ye will not tell me what you know,
But heartless, heedless leave us both to woe.
But I MUST find, MUST see my darling one;
Adieu all duties else beneath the sun!"

GOOD AND EVIL.

Idyl V.—Pride and Providence.

JUSTICE.

The rosy hours have rolled away
Another year of night and day,
And butterflies have lived and died,
And birds have caroled side by side;
Sage ants have labored hard to fill,
With winter store, their conic hill;
The dews have called the bees to roam,
And store the dulcet honeycomb;
The grass has sprung with gladness up,
And meadows nursed the Buttercup,
And flowers have climbed the mountain side,
The highest, still the soonest died;
States, nations too have scrambled high,
But states and nations often die.
If you would count, by one and one,
The labors which this year has done;
The little joys of life and love;
The green below, the bright above;
The sighings, suings, calls, and coos,
The souphs and sippings in the dews:

The tunes, and trills, and tips, and tones,
Behind the leaves, beneath the stones;
The throbbings of most loving hearts,
The curious, cunning, courting arts;
The cheering, chirping little blisses
That cling to kindnesses and kisses;
If you could count the raptures all,
In mead and mountain, hut and hall,
You must confess this year has done
Its duty full to every one.
Its roundest, richest consummation,
I will report in brief narration.

II.

In Maine there lived a Solomon,—
His patronymic, Singleton,—
He was his mother's dumpy doll,
And hence she called him SONNIE SOL.
Her usual tone was tonic A,
When Solomon was near, at play;
But if he could nowhere be seen,
She shrieked the twelve and seventeen,—
A handsome youth without a heart,
Mamma's result of woman's art;
An heir to tenements and gold,
And acres in the West untold;
But as to feeling, honor, love,
He seemed to walk one stage above;
He strutted stately,—tapp'd his boot,—
One-third immortal,—two a brute.
Ah! such a leer was in his eye,
You gazed, and yet you hurried by;

His language coarse, his pleasures low.
His voice a Siren's, in the snow.
He talked of horses, dogs, and game;
Had jokes, but always told the same ;
He was Apollo's form in stone,
Spoke ever in an under-tone ;
If blood ran in that marble form,
It ran not in a current warm.

III.

Awhile this breathing fossil drew
The kind regard of all he knew ;
The damsels loved him, every one.
So rich was Solomon in fun.
The fiftieth time his joke was utter'd.
Fresh acclamations leaped and mutter'd.
Sweet, gentle Mattie loved him first :—
She would have told him, if she durst,
He won, he left her straight away ;
Poor, weeping Mattie turned to clay.
And then the lithesome Katie Kline
Next dangled at his fishing line ;
But she was made of sterner stuff,
And bore desertion well enough,
And Minnie, Mollie, Dolly, Doe,
From fun and laughter leap'd to woe.
And Solomon, one day, averr'd,—
His mother, knitting, sat and heard,—
He said, that all the victories won
By Cæsar, Nelson, Washington,
Not half so glorious seemed to him.
As this supreme, triumphant whim

W

Of wooing, winning, breaking hearts
This game of lies and Cupid darts.
"If only I could find on earth
Some lass of real sense and worth,
Who never sighs and never loves,
Nor talks of constancy and doves,
I would secure her, hold her fast,
And find congenial charms at last."

IV.

For weeks the whisper stole abroad,
That crafty fraud might punish fraud;
That soon to see her country kin,
A belle was coming, hard to win;
The Belle of Bangor, bright and young,
With Stoic maxims on her tongue,
Who laughs at love and dying swains,
And hearts, and hopes, and tender pains;
That lawyers, doctors, half a score,
Had died rejected at her door.
Now tired of suitor and of slain,
She comes to Cumberland again,
And lads and lasses, neighbors all,
Pay Solomon a friendly call,
Suggest, applaud, impress, impart,
The hint of conquering art by art.

V.

The Belle of Bangor comes to-day;
Her cousins meet her down the way,
With gliding sleigh and tinkling bell,
And greeting smiles of welcome-well:

She leans her head,—a hint or two,
And Katie tells her what to do.
The neighbors flock to see the Fair;
Her cousins prompt with cautious care.
The trim DECEIVER, soon at hand,
Felt something hard to understand.
He tried his round of jokes again;
He faltered, simpered, tried in vain;
His accents broken, thoughts unstrung;
A strange singultus locked his tongue,
He stammered when to speak he tried,
With something throbbing at his side.

VI.

Mysterious is the origin
Of everything which must begin.
Which first,—this mystery uncoil,—
The soil, or plant which makes the soil?
A living, vegetable stock—
The lichen—grows upon the rock,
And when it dies, as die it must,
It spreads a vegetable crust.
And crops of lichens then may grow,
With air above, and soil below,
But how the parent lichen grew,
Is hard to understand, but true:
Well, how can love or feeling start,
Without a soul, without a heart?
And, with the light of love unknown,
Pray, tell us how the heart has grown?
But Solomon now felt it beat,
And all his bitter turned to sweet,

He gazed, he followed everywhere,—
Insane when absent, fool when near.
He bent above her hand one day,
And shivered as he tried to say :
" I love you, darling, more and more!"
The Beauty screamed, amid the roar
Of all the gay, astonished crowd ;
Then stood agaze, and cried aloud,
" You, Sonnie!—love!—You, hope for me,
The rival of your hounds to be!
No, Solomon! Expect to wed
Some ladie-love without a head,
For, if you choose a girl of sense,
Her wit may be at your expense."
Amid the roar of cachination,
Which hailed this caustic consecration,
Sol hurried home.   He would have died,
Had Love in him supplanted Pride.

TRUST.

The land, the land, where the lightest sound
  Will reach the hills afar,
Mysterious echoes bound, rebound,
  Like rush of distant car ;
Where stones unhewn in complets stand
  Above the nameless dead,
The long-drawn Wadi, lined with sand,
  With Rittem white bespread,—
There grows the sacred Seyaleh,
In yellow reaches of the day.

Ah, me!—what memories linger here,
   By Palm and Tarfa tree!
What classic grace, what lonely fear,
   In Wady Ta-i-beh!
Thou hoary Past—thou living ray,
   More sacred than the dawn,
Re-light the long-departed day,
   The golden ages gone,
When men of truth, and men of trust,
Believed the law that God is just.

To wild Arabia's burning shore,
   A wandering Hebrew came,
Condemned to see his home no more,
   Or curse the Christian name;
And now the star of peace began
   To kindle in the sky,
When, lo, the solitary man,
   Beheld a village nigh,
For, "God," he said, "is kind and true,
And best he knows what best to do!"

'T was Christmas Eve, and mirth profane,
   Inspired the village throng;
The Hebrew sought repose in vain,
   The noisy streets along.
From banquet-room and bridal hall,
   The revelry came down,
They mocked the stranger's humble call,
   And drove him from the town.
"But God," he said, "is just and true,
And best he knows what best to do!"

Beneath a neighboring hill he found
    Some refuge for the night ;
His dog and mule were ranged around,
    His lamp supplied him light.
Alas! the howling tempest blew,
    His lamp refused to shine,
Nor could the lonely man review,
    The word of Grace divine.
"But God," he said, "is wise and true,
And best he knows what best to do!"

But ere he sought reprieve in sleep,
    And ere he knelt to pray,
A wolf voracious, from the steep,
    Had torn his dog away.
"Dark is my fate," the exile said,
    "And darker seems to grow,
My fond, my faithful friend is dead,"
    And tears unbidden flow.
"But God," he said, "is good and true,
And best he knows what best to do."

That moment from the briery dale,
    Wild as the hills they rule,
Two panthers, leaping on the trail,
    Devoured his weary mule.
"Alas! alas!" the wanderer cries,
    "What hope or refuge now ?
How shall I leave these torrid skies,
    This mountain's burning brow ?
But God is holy, great, and true,
And best he knows what best to do."

IDYL V.   GOOD AND EVIL.

Morn came.   The holy man of God
  The festive town regained,
The merry streets he lately trod,
  No reveller contained ;
All bloody were the painted walls,
  The bridal chamber bare,
And death had filled the banquet halls,—
  For robbers had been there.
"Oh!   God!" he cries, "most just and true,
Thou knowest best what best to do!

"Had I been welcomed here to share
  These people's feast so gay,
Like them I should be weltering there,
  In wounds and death to-day.
Or had my lamp been seen afar,
  My dog or mule been heard,
This body on yon rocky spar,
  Would feast the wandering bird ;
Great God of Abraham, just and true
Thou knowest best what best to do!"

Strange compensations rule the scales
  Of Good and Evil here,
If now the burning Sand prevails,
  Some Oasis is near.
The roaming Arab never prays
  On Serbal's barren brow,
He finds the myrtle shade, and pays
  In peace his morning vow ;
He asks no universal green,
While lucid skies above are seen.

In vain the rosy vale regret
   When lovelier far to view,
Wide o'er the traveler's head is set
   A tent of matchless blue.
Within the Desert's silence drear,
   There smiles a "Vale of Rest,"
And where the barren Sands appear
   Lies Araby, "The Blest,"
The cedar and the pine may wave
Above the Arab's lonely grave.

No Ill is found unmingled here,
   The Prophet understood,
For Marah grows the Gurchud near,
   The Manna falls for food.
For every star that sets, you gain
   A brighter in the East;
The mountain shall become a plain,
   The Desert land a Feast,
And Nature's laws will yet retrieve
The wise who trust, the good who grieve.

GOOD AND EVIL.

Idyl VI.—The Wranglers.

THE SWORD.

I may not tread the halls to day.
   Lit up from many a valiant brow ;
Too fresh the glow, too strong the ray.
   It would but glare and glitter now.

The bard of future years will drink
   From these his fervency and flame,
And wreathe the cordon, link by link,
   That binds us to immortal fame.

My song recalls a different theme,
   And mirthful memory laughs to see
Good Farmer Furrow with his team,
   Encountering criminative Fee.

Quite lately, when the sun was low
   Upon the pathless blue,
Out through the fields I wandered slow,
   As chance or fancy drew.

The birds were twittering in the glade,
   And men were at their ploughs,
While here and there a country maid
   Was driving home the cows.

Down by a distant fallow-ground,
　　A brisk contention grew;
I listened well to catch the sound,
　　And still approaching drew.

A point for reconnoisance gained,
　　Behind a giant tree,
The myst'ry seem'd at once explained,
　　It was notorious Fee.

His left hand bore the garbage dry
　　Of documents inane,
While with his right he brandish'd high
　　His demonstrative cane.

Just o'er the fence stood Furrow mute,
　　Beside his kindred plough,
The ripening blush of rural fruit,
　　Was spreading o'er his brow;

And if your disputative share
　　Unbind his quiet breast,
You meet the wasp of wisdom there,
　　The keenest and the best.

Well, Fee was striking deep and strong,
　　In periods pruned with care:
"What is this war?" he roll'd along,
　　"This war of hound and hare?

We send our armies o'er the bound
　　Which natural Justice drew,
And blood and ashes heaped around,
　　The groaning lands bestrew."

But Furrow's visage kindled now,
    His soul consents to glow ;
He leaps instinctive on his plough,
    And words begin to flow.

Why, sir, we tear those people free
    From cruel lords and base,
And brighter views of liberty
    Exalt that mongrel race ;

And purer principles divine,
    Of mercy, grace, and truth,
O'er all those Papal spires will shine
    To light their rising youth.

O yes!—when neighbor Broomfield's wife
    Gets in her fit of ire,
Hurls at his head her vengeful knife,
    His bank-bills in the fire!

If then he venture but to hold
    Her hands from doing harm,
The dames around, both young and old,
    All shudder with alarm.

They peel his name, they plague his heart
    With "cruel,—cruel man!"
Unless he let his weaker part
    Just do whate'er she can."

Now this completely fail'd to please,
    Foe's mind began to roam,
And brood on curtain homilies,
    So often heard at home.

"But think, good Furrow, only think!
　Your treasury is dry,
And daily drain'd, the streams must sink.
　Your honest toils supply.

Our slaughtered friends, our chiefs forsooth,
　Lie heedless of their fame,
While many a stout and sturdy youth,
　Must drag a mangled frame.

"O glorious land!—illustrious year!"—
　Glad Furrow here rejoins,—
"What have our rulers now to fear
　From lack of blood or coins?

Arm'd with the sword, one gentle hand,
　Has wrought condign redress,
The other fed a starving land
　And banished her distress.

But had our people, cold to fame,
　Refused our wrongs to right,
E'en you would call them timorous, tame,
　The slaves of fear and fright.

Do what we may, some folks will chide;
　If seen on foot,—we're poor;
But if with stirrups bless'd, we ride,
　"You're proud," says every boor.

Some people too are rack'd with pain,
　If but a cricket sings,
And deem they hear a ghost complain
　In every bell that rings.

'Tis said that once a Grecian swain,
  Who shook to see a scar,
Resolved at last on one campaign
  And hasten'd for the war.

The camps were nigh,—a raven croak'd,—
  He paused in long dismay;
But having all the gods invok'd,
  Once more resum'd his way:

A second croak!—he turned and fled,
  Back for his home amain;—
"You shall not have my flesh," he said,
  "Your croaking is in vain."

And YOU, who all this stuff advance,
  Against the war and Polk,
I surely think this day perchance,
  You heard a raven croak."

But yet our son of Themis burn'd
  To urge his proofs again;
Alas! the rail beneath him turn'd,
  And down he pitch'd amain.

Kind Furrow soon had promptly run,
  His ready aid to yield,
But foaming, frighten'd at the fun,
  His horses scour the field.

And there was Fee, non-suited, low,
  Wide-sprawling where he fell;
And leaving Furrow shouting—"wo!"
  I ran away to tell.

THE MITRE.

Hold, Reverends, hold! 't is reason's, nature's plea;
Fierce Torry, Chambers, bend the plastic knee;
Armed with the Bible, legates of the Lamb,
'T is yours to preach, and bid the world be CALM;
Poor sinners tremble when your voices rise,
And ladies love your SANCTIMONIOUS eyes;
Ye preach of patience, charity, and love,
And dove-eyed Peace—ye woo her from above,
But if the weary, or the wicked doze,
Before your sermons reach the ling'ring close,
Your hearts with holy indignation swell,
And wakening culprits feel the fires of Hell.
Be patient now!—a sinner would beseech,
And hear, for once, an humble sinner preach;
I am too bold—I dread my daring flight,
Yet Conscience tells me that my cause is right.
I shrink, believe me, as I try to climb
The blazing summit of your souls sublime;
And as I creep around the lofty verge,
And look within upon that boiling surge,
Where Envy, Malice, holy Hate, and Fear,
Lie rankling, reeking on the billows drear;
I almost fancy that must be the Hell,
Of which the Scriptures and your sermons tell.
Too daring thus, unconscious why, or how,
The bold adventurer climbs to Ætna's brow,
Darts from the crater and the lurid fires,
Or fond, like Pliny, lingers and expires.

Oh! think, remember! when WE go astray,
When passions blind, or pleasure's toys betray,
When vulgar oaths profane the sacred air,

Or muttering drunkards reel away dull care;
When wives are frighten'd, when the children squall,
And half Rag-Alley mingles in the brawl:
Or when pale Want purloins some puny pin,
Or yielding Beauty first consents to sin,
Your holy Reverence shuns that guilty ground;
You pout your labials, in a sneer profound;
Ye dress your periods with the direful fate,
Of those who wrangle, but who seldom HATE:
Ye drill your odium on the public mind,
And interdict the kindness of the kind;
Ye tear the vail that hangs at Mercy's door,
To hide the frail offences of the poor.

But ye! Oh, ye! can let your holy ire,
Inflaming, set the WIDOW'S WEEDS on fire,
Till hollow murmurs from the dead repair,
To curse your envy, and deplore your prayer.
Yes;—ye can shrug your shoulders at another,
And DOUBT if ye may dare INVITE a brother,
While e'en the sacred desk can scarce conceal,
The winks ye wish another's heart to feel:
Yes; ye can stake a future Hell to win,
Not guilt and folly from the paths of sin,
Not reckless wretches from the lawless deed,
But wealthy Elders from a rival's creed.

And must we read each charge, and each reply?
Still hear your Reverence give and take the lie?
How can we spare the mitre, or the gown,
When slang and slander inundate the town?
How can we kneel with fervent heart to pray,
Or trust the Faith your reckless broils betray?

Oh! sacred Truth! Oh, charity! declare,
Is this Religion, this the heavenly Fair?
Who smiled on Judah in the days of Eld,
Whom Mithra's priests from Iran's hills beheld?
Is this the spirit that inspired the dove,
O'er Jordan's waters with the voice of love;
That holy Pneuma which forever flows,
And no man wisteth how it comes or goes,
Still breathing, stealing, warming, kindling through,
The depths of Nature and of Feeling too;
Which makes our being bless the mystic tie,
That links all spirits through the earth and sky:
The bond of friendship, home, and social bliss,
The bond that binds us to a world like this;
The thrill that sweetens all the ills of clay,
That makes us bless the darkness and the day;
Gives truth to science, loveliness to art,
Roars in the thunder, whispers in the heart,
Smiles in our gladness, pities in our sighs,
Pleads in the Bible, beckons in the skies?
Say, have ye felt this all-pervading Power,
Steal through your being in some hallowed hour?
Oft have ye felt it, but ye feel no more;
That thrill is gone; will not your pride deplore?
Oh! seek it not in that malignant breast!
The Dove divine must have a downy nest:
And having sought, and vainly woo'd it long,
Oh! deem not then your Paynim preacher wrong.

GOOD AND EVIL.

Idyl VII.—Kalonimata.

SALLIE.

Starry mansions, cycladean,
  Take my dearest. It is best.
Would I close the Empyrean?
  Would I keep her from the Blest?
    She so musically bright,
    Moulded, not of clay, but light,
    Here amused, detained too long,
    Wintry world of ruth and wrong.
Oh! the bliss, to whisper—"Sallie!"
  Name to me forever dear;
She, the rosiest of the Valley;
  I but whisper'd;—she was near!

Bliss! to walk the fragrant alley;
  Meet the moon, the morn with her;
Read old Ossian, weep Sunmalla,
  Dash the glistening gossamer;
    Kiss her,—lip, and cheek, and brow,
    All in dust and darkness NOW;—
    THEN the clay that charmed my sight,
    Light around this "child of light."
        Y.

"Lay me,"—spoke the voice beside me,—
"Lay me in yon Walnut shade,
When the fragrant turf must hide me;
When the holy rites are paid."

Now, my Naiad hath allied me,
Tied me to this Walnut shade;
Nymphs, your choicest blooms provide me;
Loveliest spot shall this be made.
And I know that Nature too,
Will rejoice to bloom for you,
Pansies fresh and free bestow,
Proud of hallowed dust below.
She was lovely; angels know it;
And I loved her; angels know;
Let my soul—this dust below it—
Drain to dregs the bliss of woe.

Deep reversion;—deep I owe it,
Paid it since the hour we met;
Love may bring;—if heaven bestow it,
Raptures Love can ne'er forget.
Does not love,—eternal Love,
Spirit-missioned from above,
Take the dust, the drop, the dew,
Glorify them, through and through,
Light with rapture, fill with song,
Radiate with memories strong,
Lay them down—the dear, the true,
Hallow'd dust, and hallow'd dew!
While the deathless Sallie, fleeting
From this Psyche of the earth,
Hears the great Pleroma greeting,
And an angel springs to birth.

TEXANA.

Soft glanced her fingers, white and round,
    In light along the keys,
And from the chords came swarms of sound,
    Melodious atomies,
Bright winged Ariels, golden, gay,
    With voice of life and love,
Revel'd in rosy tides of day,
    And smiled around, above.

In bounding bliss the quaver rose,
    The crotchet, minim, breve,
And Time and Mode, with bar and close,
    Would brook no false reprieve.
The grace, grupette, staccato, trill,
    The Dorian, Lydian mood,
And sense and soul, in warbling thrill,
    Leaped from their solitude.

My soul became a quaver too,
    Among the quavers there,
I talked with spirits old and true,
    Immortal now and fair;
I met Rossini, Herz, and Strauss,
    All breathing, bright again,
Tired of the grave, the "narrow house,"
    Each trill'd his master strain.

We talked of years, the old, the new,
    We talked of youth and love,
Of smile and vow—the fond, the true,
    Called to the light above.

We talked of melody and power,
  Emotion, thought divine,
Of Teian and Castalian bower,
  Of Sirens, Muses nine.

And then they formed a wreath of light,
  Around Texana's brow,
And kissed the lines of memory bright,
  That graced her beauty now.
My soul—yet unimmortalized,—
  Dared not to venture there;
It stood in transports, harmonized,
  But only stood to stare.

Hail! power divine—celestial art!
  Mysterious charm of sound!
Call back the memories of the heart,
  Unclose the grave profound.
For, at thy touch of magic skill,
  The souls of "long ago,"
Breathe, with our fair Texanas still.
  Immortal life below.

ALDINE.

Melodious Aldine, comrade of the brave!
Weep for the land thy valor could not save;
Weep for the dead,—the NAMELESS DEAD who lie,
Untomb'd, unknown, beneath the weeping sky;
Thy pensive strain, their monument shall be,
Strong as their spirits, now redeem'd and free.
Their noble deeds, with truth and music told,
Will ask no fane, no pyramid of gold;
Their memories, shrin'd in classic verse, shall find,
A fadeless mausoleum in the mind.

And daughters, bid to twine the anadem,
Will know thy Muse hath sung it all for them ;
And blasted hopes, and bleeding hearts will see
Sons, brothers, fathers half-restored in thee.

O, sweet belief! unbodied spirits know
Our hopes, our fears, our sympathies below.
From rosy climes, from regions pure and free,
They stoop, they love their mortal walks to see ;
Through twilight shades on viewless wings deploy,
Hear every sigh, and note each rising joy ;
O'er mother, maidens, sisters, lovers lean,
Breathe, murmur, sigh, immortal sighs, unseen.
With fragrant airs they fan the fever'd cheek,
And, voiceless, through thy vocal numbers speak,
Bless the sweet bard who hath a tear to give,
For lovers dead, and hopeless loves that live.

Alas! how few in this degenerate clime,
Will prize the pathos of thy polished rhyme!
The worth of steed and carriages we know,
Of satin snood, of silken furbelow ;
Too hard for us o'er metaphors to think,—
Fill high the bowl! Our business is to drink ;
Too hard for us to make a SMALL ADVANCE,—
Trip high the heel! Our business is to dance.

Dull Pride, the illegitimate of Hate,
Counts not your syllables, if ten or eight ;
Counts his broad acres, counts his coins galore,
Nor heeds the orphan wailing on the shore ;
That skull,—alas! poor man, I knew him well,
His wife, his child, his cottage by the fell.
He came to see them :—lingered but a day ;
The bloated landlord order'd him away :

Pale mothers, shivering in the wintry dell,
Fond sisters, wandering oft to flood and fell,
"To camp! to camp! thy more befitting sphere."
He went—he battled:—lo! his skull is here!
Bless'd with no tomb, no monumental stone,
Bless'd with the bard's immortal Dirge alone.

MARY.

Sweet vision of that spirit view!
   It wrapp'd my heart in bliss;
I trod, methought, beyond the blue,
   A purer world than this.
I saw a loftier, lovelier sky,
   And flowers of fadeless stem;
There came a thought—I knew not why,
   A thought of Bethlehem.

And then a dear one told me there,
   It was a bliss to die—
"Through gloom I broke, pain, hope, despair,
   And found this world, this sky!
O! blest the father, mother be!
   Go, tell my joy to them:
They link'd my name and memory
   With HERS of Bethlehem.

"And through my score of earthly years,
   A dearer memory came,
The life I read with love and tears,
   Messiah's holier name.
For Fancy, Memory, Love divine,
   Would wreathe a paradem,
And MARY was the braid to twine
   The flowers of Bethlehem.

Tell him who gave his heart to me,—
　The fond, the true, the brave;
Tell him I saw his agony,
　Whilst bending o'er my grave.
This amaranthine wreath I twine,
　For him this anadem,
His MARY sends the gift divine,
　In dews of Bethlehem.

TILLIE.

She reach'd the golden hills of youth,
A feeble, beauteous child of clay,
Reach'd e'en the bays of classic Truth,
And sweetly tuned to grave or gay,
Her cheerful wisdom woo'd the heart away.

My days with her were like a shining river,
Alas! too brief, but grateful to the Giver.
They drank her smile, but soon that smile was clouded
I bathed in love, but love itself was shrouded;
Leave me to mourn, for mourning is a pleasure,
Down in the grave I laid my darling treasure,
And Memory waits my days and nights to measure.

Pure, crystal Night—prophetic Night!
Reveal the star where TILLIE dwells;
I ask but one delicious sight—
Can all your everlasting wells,
Effuse the bliss, that with her memory swells?

ESTALINE.

　A rhyme! a rhyme for ESTALINE!
　I want a rhyme for ESTALINE.
　Oh! light this pleasing task of mine,
　　To find a rhyme for Estaline.

Why, Nature all from bird to bower,
From hill to dale, from mead to flower,
From azure hill to crystalline,
Is proud to rhyme with Estaline.
Her name, her voice, each sigh or sign,
All sweetly rhyme with Estaline.
Out stroll the swains at early dawn,
Thro' street, and lane, and mead, and lawn,
What makes them look so blithe and fine;
Their spirits rhyme with Estaline.
The woodbine, vine, and eglantine, —
Lo! how they rhyme with Estaline!
The Crystalline, the Apennine, —
The mountains rhyme with Estaline
The Saline, Sabine, Philippine, —
The islands rhyme with Estaline,
The winding Mayne, the lovely Rhine,
The rivers rhyme with Estaline.
The wealth, the brightness of the mine,
Are rich in rhymes for Estaline;
From stars to jewels—all that shine,
Delight to rhyme with Estaline.

Ah! should the eye of ENVY fall,
Upon this rough and rugged scrall,
Why would she flout the votive line?
SHE does not rhyme with Estaline.
And all that's fair, and pure, and fine.
Will harmonize with Estaline.
Because a tender, generous heart,
A bosom void of guile or art,
Spread o'er the face a charm divine,—
All pure things rhyme with Estaline.

GOOD AND EVIL.

Idyl VIII.—Passing Away.

KAGEY—"THE GOOD MAN."

Come, meekest virgins of the vale,
   With silent step and votive tear,
With cypress boughs and pansies pale,—
   Your Abdiel is sleeping here,
From Pennsylvania's epic shades,
   Where first the paths of life he trod,
Sweet Ephratah, thy vestal maids,
   Bedew this consecrated sod :—
What Elah that the prophets knew,
On holier ground its shadow threw?

Come see where now the mantling snow,
   One spot with whitest swell invests ;—
Here with his children deep below,
   In silent happiness he rests.
Ay, purer than the snow that heart,
   Which meekly lies unthrobbing here ;
More undefiled the god-like part
   He bore in our precarious sphere,
And deathless in our souls shall be
The fragrance of his memory.

Z

The breezes of suspiring Spring
   From Massanutten's side shall blow,
Around this spot their incense fling,
   And sigh in holy whispers low;
For while with joyful haste he trod,
   Yon deapening dale and arduous hill,
The conscious, all-pervading God
   Engrossed his soul-felt whispers still,
And still the airs of hill and plain,
Effusions from his lips retain.

In yonder lane the widow lorn,—
   Naomi of our heartless years,—
Leans o'er her orphans every morn,
   And yields to unavailing tears;
For, he whose voice had soothed so long
   Sad memory's unobtrusive sigh,
Whose hand secured from reckless wrong,
   Whose bosom bled at sorrow's cry,
He too has left our wintry shore,—
He hears the sufferer plead no more.

Ah! never down the rocky vale
   She hastes to meet her orphan's more;
Shares the warm kiss and lifts the pail,
   White-wreathed with sweetness from his store.
No more the fatherless from play,
   Shall run with lisping joy to tell,—
"The good man brings his gifts to day;
   Come see his white locks in the dell."
Deep Death hath wrapped in darkness now,
The honors of that reverend brow.

Long years through flood and beating storm,
    The messenger of life divine,
We saw his worn and wasting form
    Expanding still his blest design ;
Age came with mortal omens sere,
    Keen Pain, and Blindness, and Decay ;
Though clouded in his high career,
    The glorious watchman spurned delay ;
Through dark'ning years, wrapt echo rung
The dictates of his fervent tongue.

And when from each familiar aisle,
    Inveterate Time his feet withdrew,
E'en strangers paused to share his smile,
    And learn submission sweet and true.
As ling'ring years subdued his frame,
    Still warmer grew the whispered prayer ;
Till silence o'er his chamber came ;
    The shadow of White Death was there ;
Wan daughters ceased their watch to keep,
And strangers turned away to weep.

Cease, meekest virgins of the vale !
    Dim not with tears your Abdiels's tomb ;
Fond spirit of the choral gale,
    Thy starlit wing of Faith resume !
He has rejoined the countless throng,
    That glow in unapparent space ;
Sweet on his lips triumphant song,
    Ethereal beauty on his face,
And radiant with Immortal youth,
He wings the realms of love and Truth.

THE MINSTREL.

Summer breeze and fragrance, wooing,
  Call me to the hills again :
Tender turtles still are cooing ;
  Still, sweet Lynville, still complain ?
Shades of Edom, come around me,
  Windy hill and winding dale !
Long ago your voices bound me ;
  Oh ! the distant years,—how pale !
    I, a laden Memory, roaming,
    Sorrows past around me gloaming.

Where, ye beams, ye birds, ye breezes,
  All the beauty, bliss of then ?
Wandering, warming, where it pleases,
  Round the homes of other men ?
Would ye mind me of the former ?
  Dear ye are, but dearer they ;
Memory makes them hollier, warmer,
  Lonely, lost, and far away,
    Full of bliss and full of sorrow ;
    O, my yesterday ! My morrow!

If some wall of fate should sever
  All the Good from all the Ill ;
Life forbid, and death, forever,
  Each the other's place to fill,
How would Change, sweet source of pleasure,
  Mitigate a world like this ?
Sound and silence make the measure ;
  Good and evil make the bliss ;
    And nocturnal revelations
    Supplement the sun's ovations.

Hark!—from all the dale below me,
  Choral bursts of voices swell:—
Sing, sweet choristers! bestow me
  Tones and memories loved so well!
Gone?—O, no; the Minstrel liveth;
  Soul and song can never die;
Spirit taketh, spirit giveth
  Life from Edens in the sky,
    And the deathless, full fruition
    Kindleth all our inanition.

Pride of life and love, to rally,
  In the fane of song divine,
Young creations of the valley,
  Round a soul-devoted shrine;
Fire each heart with new emotion;
  Warm it, mould it, make it feel
Seraph lapses of devotion,
  Which symphonious tones reveal,
    Lapses of the bliss eternal,
    Dripping from the veil supernal.

Nothing dies; it only passes,
  Like the hills which I have trod;
Lives are but mysterious glasses,
  Linking all our days to God.
And the Good Old Man is living,
  In the young, the fond, the fair,
Life melodious drinking, giving
  Down the chords of light and air,
    Minstrel of the mountain heather,
    We shall always live together.

ERASMUS.

I had one hope, one human solace left,
Laid up for life's gray years. But long, my son!—
It seems an age of inauspicious dream,—
Since last in joy we met, when absence brief
Had made our meeting dearer to the heart;
Since last I saw,—delusive phantoms all :—
In thy dear smile the orient light of youth,
Saw Joy, and Health, and fresh impulsive Life,
Kindling with all the rosy flush of soul,
Thy form and face, my sweetly pensive boy!
Who did not love thee? But too deep our love,
So deep, it mingled all our bliss with fear:—
A sadly sweet and melancholy joy.
And we are now so desolate—so long
Waiting in loneliness and silence here,
Waiting to speak with thee. O come, my son:
For I have marked full many a glowing page,
Pregnant with meaning, rich with holy thought,
Ambrosial food for spirits pure as thine.

Sweet hours, my son! delicious hours we knew,
And bright conceptions cast their light around.
We loved to range the immaterial realm,
To talk of spirit and ethereal mind,
Its destiny, its principles, its powers,
Its dawning aspirations, hopes, and loves,
And moving sympathies, and blameless joys;
Its sentiments of loveliness and grace;
Faith, Reason—sister denizens of heaven.

But, woe is me! Thou comest now no more,
To intertwine thy purity of thought.
They tore thee from my home and heart away,

My soul is joyless,—at this bleeding heart,
Sad pulses keep a painful throbbing still.
My treacherous hopes have vanished;—dark the morn
And in the midnight hour unquiet thrown,
I hear the sounding coach go by, nor feel
The touch of that dear hand, whose touch was bliss.
The cherish'd purpose of my life is gone;
My fondest labor sleeps suspended now.
How can I think, unless in hope to share
The bliss or beauty of each thought with thee!
Why should I twine my sorrows into song,
Unless thou read the melancholy strain!
The noisy world goes on, and nature wears
A wintry aspect all the weary year.
Oh! I am lonely in this bleak abode,
This gloom invokes the lustre of thy smile;
This silence woos the music of thy voice;
But woos, alas! invokes and woos in vain?

The heart, the heart!—triumphant alchemist,—
Refines a toy, turns pebbles into gems,
This book, this little knife, those sketches rude—
First essays of thy hand—could all the gold,
Which despots wring from starving serfs replace?
These are my dearest symbols of the past;
Symbols of thee, and youth, and health, and hope,—
The golden links of that mysterious chain,
Our telegraph, which mounts to thee and heaven.
Thy desk is near me, near me still the spot,
Where thou did'st kindle in the Mantuan lay,
In sweetest tones, attune to modern phrase,
The smooth rotundity of Tully's sense,
The liquid cadence of Venusian odes.

I must awake from this bewildering dream,
Why should I wait to hear that voice again,
Moulding the atmosphere that mortals breathe.
Dear faces still surround me—faces dear
To thee; but never can that placid brow
Reflect again the light of yonder sun.
And I "must bear it:"—this was thy behest,
When in my soul's deep agony, those lips
Subsiding into silence, whisper'd soft
The counsel of a Christian,—"Try to bear."
Sweet names each day are utter'd in my ear,
But one dear name I hear them call no more,
It has a meaning deeper than we deem'd,—
Erasmus, THE BELOVED ONE,—too deep,—
For us too holy; angels speak it now.
And I would gladly lay this broken frame
Beside thy slumbering dust; enough of earth,
Its real woes and visionary joys!
I feel a trembling trust, the Bright and Blest
Of that fair clime where thou art smiling now,
Would not disdain the presence of a suppliant;
To let him hear once more that sacred name,
That spirit tone, and look in those dear eyes,
Radiant with rapture and the light of heaven.

GOOD AND EVIL.

Idyl IX.—Behind the Veil.

CRAMER.

Here, amid the climes diurnal,
    Just before the veil I wait,
Soon to hear the voice Supernal
    Sounding through the vaults of Fate ;
Soon, sweet Hope, immortal youth,
Leaping from the shrine of Truth,·
Woo each warm anticipation
O'er the portals of sensation.

Did Jehovah but design me
    For a moment's dream of time?
To these perishing joys confine me,
    Barr'd from yon eternal clime?
Is this musing mind a breath,
Lost in all—victorious death,
Frail as dust and vapor flying,
When these mortal powers are dying?

Soon this frame will be a plunder,
    Crumbling for the worms below ;
Must I, as it sinks asunder,
    All to mold'ring darkness go ?
&

All of conscious life bereft,
At my utmost limit left,
Born to quench each warm sensation,
Deep in drear annihilation?

Is not life a path allow'd me,
  Up to life beyond the sky?
Why hath God with thought endow'd me,
  If the powers of thought must die?
Happy, were I made to be,
Like the brute from reason free,
Gay amid the seasons o'er me,
Heedless of the doom before me.

No;—reviler! scorn and error
  Ne'er shall steal my trust away;
Rescued, raised from mortal terror,
  I shall triumph o'er decay.
No;—my soul is not a breath,
Not the passive prey of death;
From my Maker I enjoy it,
Storms of Fate shall not destroy it.

Spirit!—that's my name imperial,
  Clay is but a cumbrous pall,
But the seed of life ethereal,
  Slumbering for the trumpet's call.
As the glad maternal earth
Warms the genial seed to birth,
So this frame to dust descending,
Shrines the germ of life unending.

Not for momentary being,
  Cursed with consciousness in vain;
Not for joys forever fleeing;
  Not for throbs of guilt and pain,

He hath made this soul for bliss,
Harmonized her powers for this,
Winged each Godlike aspiration
O'er the bourne of desolation.

This warm thirst for life eternal,
   This impatience here to stay,
Longing for a home Supernal,
   Blissful Regions far away,
These, bright world, my tokens be,
Tokens that I rise to thee,
Burst the coils I strive to sever,
Wing me there, and live forever.

Deep remorse for deeds unholy!
   Sweet repose the righteous know!
Joys, that cheer the meek and lowly!
   Stealing down unseen below!
Vouch ye, too, this truth to me,
When the shades of Death I see,
When these limbs to worms are given,
I shall rise, and soar to heaven.

I shall live, live on forever!
   Immortality is sure!
Lo! I strive these bonds to sever,
   Bursting from a dream impure.
Let me then, to Virtue true,
Silently her path pursue,
Moving firm, with glad persistence,
Living here for yon existence.

Let thy mercy, Lord, restore me,
   When my feeble feet may roam;
Keep the joyous thought before me,—
   "Yonder is my native home!

Void of sorrow, void of pain,
There delights and glories reign,
There, before the throne suspended,
Wreath and crown of perils ended."

HOLBACH.

Pangs of rueful anguish darted,—
  Tore me in that last distress;
Earth, and sun, and sky departed,
  Deep in cold unconsciousness;
And I fancied soon to be
All from sense and sufferance free,
Atoms winnowed in the breezes;
Void of life and life's diseases.

Soul a fiction,—God a fable,
  Millions I had made to see;
Mock'd, disproved, with logic able,
  Dreams of immortality;
Clear deductions, safe and sure,—
Minds gigantic felt secure;
And the Halls of pride and station
Echoed with congratulation.

How is this?—I find me living,
  Breathing, gazing, musing still!
Gone, foregone the old misgiving,
  Gone perversities of Will!
Where the livid hands that gave
Sad forebodings of the grave?
Oh!—the flush of youth is o'er me,
Fresh existence all before me!

Mazed, I roll a keener vision
    Broad beneath the shining cope ;
Not a shade of indecision
    Rests upon the wing of Hope.
This is not the lucid blue,
Spread above the world I knew !
No ;—a canvas, crimson, golden,
Skies emerging from the olden !

Yellow clouds with brazen faces,
    Crown the amplitudes of air ;
Down the warm, eternal spaces,
    Shadows gaze, and lightnings glare :
Yet the airs are sweet around ;
Soft, melodious every sound ;
Spirits pause and look with sorrow,
In a world that hath no morrow !

See ! Yon blazing sun is stealing
    Far behind the hills away ;
There, another sun is wheeling
    Up the vault of endless day ;
And I see their beams intwine
Blazing on the crystalline,
Sending down a strong emotion,
Sweetly melting to devotion.

Thoughts, volitions, light-invested,
    Flow forever, not unseen,
Soon in vocal forms attested,
    Bringing tears and smiles between ;
Rising, passing ;—see them shine
Radiant from their source divine,
Like the sunlit mists in motion
O'er an unapparent ocean.

Eloquence! Surpassing wonder;
  Winds and waters talk of love!
I can understand the thunder,
  And the murmuring clouds above!
Sweeter language than I knew
Breathed in earthly interview,
Like a distant curfew blending
With the shouts of labors ending.

Strains of reminiscence flowing,
  Deeply trickle through the air;
In the vocal zephyrs blowing,
  Whisper wisdom in my hair;
Dear disciples I had known,
Pass, repass,—afar—alone—
Heed no token, heed no praying,
On! away!—no step delaying.

Dual sunbeams sympathetic,
  Strike this lute, which seems divine;
From the chords in light magnetic,
  O, the words that answer mine!
And sweet Echo, pensive child,
Rings the words in mountains wild,
Rings the chords, elastic, shining,—
Mystic tones of love repining.

Oh! the cruelty of kindness!
  Oh! the sting of each reply!
Curses on my stony blindness;—
  See, and feel,—and yet deny!
ALIM, heaving mountains, seas,—
ADONAI, in flowers and trees,—
ELOI, from the stars appealing,—
GOD, within the soul revealing!

Heart, my heart! remorse is bitter!
　　Love was in my nature too;
I could find the wiser, fitter,
　　Why not find the PRIMAL TRUE?
Find her in the fields of light,
Find her in the crystal night,
Ere the searcher, lost forever,
Felt the worm that ceases never.

I could love the rich, the real,
　　Sunny fields of science try,
Find within the blue ideal,
　　Worlds beyond my native sky:
Fail, alas! still fail to see
MORAL worlds of purity,
Worlds of righteous Law and Duty,
Interwoven with the Beauty!

Light I saw,—no luminary;
　　Love without the Spring of love;
Life without its commentary;
　　Truth below, no Truth above;
Knew the just, the wise, the free,
Felt the Right—the OUGHT TO BE,
Swam the Universal River,
Saw no Fountain, found no Giver!

Fool to love the forms of Beauty,
　　Not the Light that makes the Fair;
Fool, to feel a sense of Duty,
　　Not the Pure which brought it there!
Fool, to greet the Graces Three,
Not Idothea by the Sea,
Nurse my dream of drear Nirvanna,
While the angels shout Hosanna!—

Dreams of drear annihilation,
    While the Magi pour the myrrh,
While the shepherds feel salvation
    All the wells of being stir!
But I find He can forgive;
Now I know Him;—still I live,
Still remorse from memory borrow,
Drain my Alcahest of sorrow!

Vivid, flashing intuitions,
    Strangely link'd with Reason here,
Sever Essences—Conditions,
    And the truth of things appear.
Mind is BEING, seen in sooth;
Faith is Reason—Reason, Truth,
Life and Love,—immortal Essence
Shining in the Omnipresence.

IDOTHEA

III.

YONDER!

OR

THE BEAUTY OF HOLINESS.

קדשו סההוו בו קדוש אבו
Leviticus.

Holy be ye, for, Holy am I.

The Power, Wisdom, Truth, and Beauty displayed in this world of visible phenomena, chiefly occupied the genius of ancient philosophy. From these, they were able to conceive the existence of a moral system, and to contemplate, with their exquisite powers, the Supreme Good, the Right, the Just. It is possible still to ascend to a World essentially spiritual, and contemplate Purity, Mercy, HOLINESS, in the Absolute. In this region the Prophets of Israel delighted to dwell.

MORE LIBERTY!

With blood-stained garlands crown for thee,
The lawless shrine of Liberty ?
Away, remorse ! regret, away !
Queen Acolasia rules the day ;
Luxurious streams of opulence,
Indulge, regale, voracious sense !
What more, full heart ?—Ah ! fill who can
The void that aches within the man !

Sweet, rosy vistas, wide withdrawn :
Aurora laughing o'er the lawn :
The free expanse of starry night,
The high, the beautiful, the bright ;
Art, Genius, charming all the day,
With Lydian air, and Orphic lay ;
What more, frail heart ?—Repose who can :
A void still aches within the man !

On thought unfetter'd, rise, and trace
Your waving curves in mind or space ;
Your spirals, cissoids interview,
Evoke the lovely from the true ;
You toil for Wisdom, not for pay,—
Thrones may not buy your heart away ;
What more, fond bosom ?—Cure who can
This void that aches within the man !

The shining fields of Nature call,
Strange powers, abysses, forces, all ;

Fresh Revelations—reeling Sense—
Rich flashes of Intelligence ;
Ethereal heights ! how blest to be
Above the world's complicity !
What more, proud bosom ?—Heal who can
The void that aches within the man !

Go, wing the depths of soul profound,
From chains material all unbound :
In light serene, ambrosial air,
Behold the shrine of Virtue fair ;
Where truth is law, and law is light,
Behold the beauty of the Right,
Enshrined amid the shining Fane,
Fair goddess of this Busyrane ;
Her Edict breathing wise behest,
Which no colliding wants molest ;
What more, calm heart ?—Deny who can,
A want still aches within the man !

Companion of the wise and free,
Oh ! lift the veil of Destiny !
Pass angels, ministers of love,
Behold the Absolute above !—
The One Supreme Imperative,
In whom the Thrones of nature live,
Who love and worship not for pay,—
As so much dole for so much day ;
Where life is love, and love is free,
The banquet of Euphrosyne ;
All wills attuned to Will Divine,
And HOLINESS the golden shrine ;
No more, full heart !—Enjoy who can
This Freedom which overflows the man.

IDOTHEA

III.

YONDER!

OR THE

BEAUTY OF HOLINESS.

EPIDOS I.—**URANOTHEN.**

EPIDOS I.—ANALYSIS.

Ordinary Powers.—Possible Powers.—Mutual Admiration.—Nature as a Whole.—Operations.—Subordinate and Final.—Contracted Views.—Universal and Limited.—Marston Hall.—England and America.—The Wounded Soldier.—Strange Power.—Palingenesis.—Return from the Heavens.

YONDER!

Epidos I.—Uranothen.

I

"Harp Elysian! wreathed with roses,
  Trembling at the softest thrill,
Where among your chords reposes
  Language for creative Will?
     Can I throw these warm desires,
     All among your golden wires,
     Till their Orphic tones shall tell
     Truths that now in darkness dwell?
Thoughts, emotions, long unspoken,
  Beckoning from the viewless shore,
Dreams and visions, wild, unbroken,
  Waiting to be wafted o'er.

"Wondrous boon! that tone and token
  Clothe the living soul unseen,
And from symbols, stone or oaken,
  Spirits learn what spirits mean!
     Here, Ionian, Lydian swell
     May inform the harp or shell,
     Natives of the molder'd brain
     Dwell within the brow again!

Here, far down the stream of ages,
  Borne from kindred spheres of mind,
Lives the wisdom of the sages
  Who have loved and led mankind.

II.

" Here, e'en I, though finite, fleeting,
  Learn to mould my thoughts in song :
Teach my heart melodious greeting,
  Grateful to the starry throng,
    I unfold the sound you heard,
    Pierce the picture, pierce the word,
    Read the fragrant, read the sweet,
    Read the dust beneath my feet :
Probe the star, the cloud, the ocean,
  Ope the vestments of the lawn,
Track the twining paths of motion,
  Pass the golden gates of dawn.

"And I feel a thought, a notion,
  Spring to life, unknown before,
And my soul, in sweet devotion,
  Learns to tremble and adore.
    Tell me how the wondrous change,
    So familiar, yet so strange,
    How a cloud, a star hath wrought
    In my soul a living thought!
Lo! while thou, my harp, art throwing
  Thought and feeling into sound,
Lo! the thoughts of God are glowing
  Into shining worlds around!

Richest harmonies are flowing,
  Down our distant prisons sent,

As the good redeem'd are going
  Up from bale and banishment.
    And the sons of God proclaim
    Who he is, and whence we came,
    Hold the Fair, the Good, the True,
    High in prospect, close in view,
While Saturnian ages rolling,
  Freely glad, and gladly free,
Feel the law of Love controlling,
  Round the goal of Destiny."

III.

" Law of Love! O, ne'er repeal it!
  Bright Idothea—lost Elaine!
Wakes my heart, and, O, I feel it
  Bathed in blissful dews again.
    Maid of evening, Maid of morn,
    Maid of Lyra, cycle-born!
    Ranging dew-lands of the West,
    Wrapp'd in Evening's purple crest,
    Heimdal Isles will claim us soon,
    Far away beyond the Moon,
Thou shalt reign in Allegewny,
  Lift old Cycle from the cars,
Harping at the feast of Luna,
  Banqueting among the stars.

" Like the rainbow by the Yuna,
  Beauteous o'er the Bleak below;
Like the blue-bell on Chamouni,
  Flowering in a world of snow;
    Thou with fleet and fairy form,
    Thou with fancies fresh and warm.

2

Thou with arm of chrysolite,
　　Thou with brow of marble white,
　　Thou with eye and heart sublime,
　　Come, reclaim our guilty clime;
Rise, in shapes ideal soaring,
　　Young and joyous, free and fair,
Come, exult for years, exploring
　　Saga Lore of earth and air.

" With thy harp forever pouring
　　Angel echoes far away,
Till the sun, at eve adoring,
　　In his bosom wrap the day.
　　　　In his bosom wrap Elaine,
　　　　Loving, leaping o'er the main,
　　　　And the orient stars shall see
　　　　Dear Elaine delivered, free;
And the Houri, and the Warden,
　　Ope the gates of light and love,
Bear thee through the Eastern Garden,
　　Through our Eden-home above.

IV.

"O, I leap the waves before thee,
　　O'er the bourn of Winter borne,
There a heart will still adore thee,
　　Which the thorns of time have torn.
　　　　I shall hear wild echoes come,
　　　　From our old prophetic home;
　　　　Waiting, hopeful, happy, free,
　　　　Happiest that I hear of thee.
I will build a bower in Aiden,
　　Beauteous bower of berylite,

Dædal gems from Hela Haden,
  Mossy seats of dolomite;
" Amaranths with fragrance laden,
  Pansies pure that never die,
All shall wait my radiant Maiden,
  Till she deign to wander by.
    Pause, Idothea, pause to see
    All my votive stores for thee.
    Will you talk with me above,
    Talk of Wisdom, Virtue, Love?
    Waken there the magic spell,
    Tell of hopes we used to tell,
    That the Son of God may see
    If we loved humility?
And Saturnian ages rolling,
  Freely glad, and gladly free,
Feel the law of Love controlling,
  Round the Goal of Destiny."

V.

" Thus discoursing, slow beside us
  Came from death to father's Hall,
Two BRIGHT FRIENDS, who have allied us
  With the wonders o'er the Wall;
    With strange mysteries of life,
    In the depths of Nature rife,
    In the heights of Being found,
    Dare we rise above the ground;
If fair Truth be still a rover,
  Winged with plumes of destiny,
Dipping, soaring like the plover,
  In, above, the cloudy sea."

Edwin paused. Illusions over;
  Listening airs stole softly by;
Orson frowning at the clover;
  Edwin smiling at the sky.
    Ah! too oft our hearts deceive;
    We are gay when others grieve,
    Cast our line in troubled seas,
    Pain when most we hope to please.
Edwin paused. His tale deferring;
  Meekly sues his reverend friend:
"Frown not on a novice erring,
  Errors in discoveries end."

" Heresies may come by hearing,
  Fatal to our Faith divine;
Faith demands a changeless bearing;
  Sacred charts have laid the line.
    Of discoveries HERE are none;
    Here Creation's work is done;
    Man's deliverance all unbought,
    This, the last his Grace hath wrought.
Never, till the grand Revision,
  Shall the good or bad arise;
All await the wise decision,
  And the life the Earth denies.

" Shun the dangerous, fierce collision
  Of Divine with human love;
Shun the painful, proud derision
  Of the Virgins wise above.
    Fill thy lamp with oil again;
    Deem all earthly wisdom vain;
    Genius, science, taste, deceive;
    Human morals grind and grieve;

Songs of Genius, soft, illusive,
  Steal the heart from Grace away;
Worship groveling, stern, exclusive,
  Best befits corrupted clay."

VI.

Thus the Pastor. Edwin meekly;
  " Not untaught in moods of mind,
Glad or gloomy, strong or weakly,
  I have felt the change you find.
    I have felt enough to know.
    That we reason wrong below;
    That our reasoning in the gloom,
    Changes here when seasons bloom.
Hence, from naught but intuition,
  Would I venture brief reply,
And, if wrong in my position,
  No obtuse believer I.

" Why this charming coalition,
  In the hues of sky and lawn?
Why this glorious exhibition,
  In the rosy-fingered dawn?
    Strange and sweet emotions swell
    From my heart's profoundest well;
    Is it wrong for me to know,
    Power of Beauty here below?
I would be no carping critic;
  I am pleased, I know not why;
And no inquest analytic,
  Shall this bliss of life deny.

" Not assumed, or parasitic,
  All spontaneous, genial, free,

Time's enraptured, mute enclitic,
  Smiling back Eternity.
    Air elastic, waves of song,
    Link this atmosphere along,
    From the joyful grove and lea,
    Thundering cloud and sounding sea!
Sure, there seems to me a duty,
  Thus instilled, around, above;
Earth is full of Song and Beauty,
  And my business is to LOVE.

"Why not blank, or brown, or sooty,
  Yon blue vault from cope to plain?
Why for Love provide a Lewti,
  If the bliss of Love is vain?
    Why made Heaven an atmosphere,
    Where soft whispers I may hear;
    Hear that "still, small voice" divine,
    Voice of Israel's God and thine?
Earth he made for what I find it;
  Let my tuneful heart adore!
Nor devise beyond, behind it,
  Some lost world I must deplore."

VII.

"From a bank beside a willow,
  Fragrant bank of Mundledale,
Whence, up-sloping like a pillow,
  Corn-rows rustled in the gale;
    ORSON rose and looked away,
    Where the sky was purpled gray;
    And the stem his foot had trod,
    Springing, gave a spiteful nod.

On his brow a hue more ashy,
  Hue of vengeance at the heart;
Glances furtive changed to flashy;
  Oft he strove, but failed to start.

"Talk, mere talk is vain and clashy;"—
  Orson's words were cramp and slow:—
"Human wit, at best, is trashy,
  And we know not what we know.
      Taught by wisdom from above,
      I had taught thee purer love,
      But this Beauty rules your breast,
      And her teaching sounds the best,
Mark you monk's-hood near the baylet,
  Then observe the lily white:
That displays one gorgeous raylet,
  This returns you all the light."

VIII.

"Let not;"—Edwin rose protesting;
  "Let not passion blind us here;
E'en the garb, thy form investing,
  I have reverenced; I revere.
      Earth hath children blest to see
      Wider fields of truth than we;
      And I venerate the voice,
      Taught to find a wiser choice;
Sad to find our words forever
  Moulding symbols that mislead;
Sad to feel that man can never
  See all sides of word or deed;

Sad to hear thy tongue dissever
  Love below from Love divine.

While the thought I would endeavor,
　　Links our lower loves with thine.
　　　　I but spoil, with feeble tongue,
　　　　Truths high Beings oft have sung,
　　　　Truths Idothea seems to know,
　　　　Caught above this world below,
　　　　Ere her harp had felt decay,
　　　　Ere its chords would wear away:
Chords of Sardel, glittering, bounding,
　　Wrought by skill to earth unknown,
Twelve Æolian sounds compounding,
　　Into one harmonious tone;

"Twelve responsive measures rounding,
　　As her plectrum softly smote,
Dulcet voice and word resounding
　　Some bright truth with every note:
　　　　And, she says, that Harp had made
　　　　Wilder echoes in the shade,
　　　　Sweeter symphonies arose,
　　　　Than terrestrial artist knows,
　　　　When, within her astral bower,
　　　　First she learned its magic power,
For, its sheen would but uncover,—
　　In that atmosphere of light—,
When the moons and rings above her,
　　Echoed from each radiant height;

"And its tones like birds would hover,
　　Warbling round on golden wing;
Murmuring love, they seemed to love her,
　　Warm as life, and fresh as Spring.
　　　　All who reach a world of bliss,—
　　　　Crown of virtuous life in this,—

Each the gift of song inspires,
Each a harp of golden wires,
And they charm the land and sea,
With spontaneous melody,
On their twinkling chords rehearse
Mysteries of this Universe ;
Every chord, she says, retaining
Memories of some distant home :
Like the ocean-shell complaining,
Its old plaint beneath the foam.

"Through yon Selva still remaining,
Once I saw her pass in light,
While the cloudy morn was raining,
And her form a radiance bright,
Come, and talk these matters o'er :
I will speak of them no more ;
Come, Idothea can explain
Truths I torture thus in vain.
Deem it not all visionary ;
Space is wide and Truth divine :
Come, and let our mystic Fairy,
Give you wilder views than mine.

"In full moon,—and moons do vary—
" Bright as day !"—we fondly say ;
But our dream is temporary,
Soon appears the golden day.
" I will come,"—and ORSON smiled,—
" Glad to prove you both too wild,
Wild with speculations vain,
Phantoms of a morbid brain.
But in all this sad delusion,
Gleams a sweet docility,

And I hold it no intrusion,
  Nothing rude to set you free."

IX.

Hawksbill, loveliest of the daughters
  Nursed within the mountain zone,
Each beside thy curling waters,
  Press'd his homeward path alone,
    Edwin thought each shining wave
    Token of approval gave;
    Streaks of golden gleam were spread,
    Up along the argent bed:
For the evening sun was flaming
  Down the azure plains of June;
Wren and thrush had ceased declaiming
  From the nuptial halls of noon.

And his hopeful fancies framing,
  Edwin mused, communing high;
Fancies up through Nature aiming,
  Wrought a light in heart and eye.
    Slowly passed he by the mill,
    Crossed a tributary rill,
    Reached a grove, whose summit made
    O'er his path a trellised shade.
Ah!—what sound his step arrested,
  Met and smote him like a blow;
Through the mountain azure-vested,
  Through the woody vale below?

Yes; again—again attested;
  Not of thunder, yet the same;
Boom on echoing boom molested
  Quicken'd step, and kindling frame.

"Sure, it is the cannon's roar,
　Thundering on the Eastern shore;
　Sons of Liberty and Truth,
　Would my days were days of youth!
William, at thy side contending,
　We would rush to Freedom's shrine;
Or, two lives together blending,
　Find a Freedom more divine."

Every sound an impulse lending,
　Every wish a vigor new,
Light the flowery slope ascending,
　Near his father's, Edwin drew.
　　Many a quaint armorial sign,
　　Spoke that house of ancient line,
　　Though no arch, no architrave
　　Proof of pride or splendor gave.
Marston, lineal Earl of Surry,
　Here had fixed his last abode,
Weary of the world's rude hurry,
　Or the fealty he owed.

Yet he loved Old England merry,
　England's laws and England's fame;
Memories still too dear to bury,
　Lived and throbb'd at England's name.
　　Here his sons had learned to toil,
　　Dress, and fence, and plow the soil;
　　And to guard the sacred spot,
　　William braved a soldier's lot.
While at home sat Marston feeding
　Hopes of reconcilement still;
But he deem'd all claim exceeding,
　That best claim—a Freeman's will.

"Dear Old England, ever leading
 Onward through the files of Fate,
Foremost where the brave are bleeding,
 Foremost where the wise debate;
  Mistress of the willing sea,
  Mother of the nations free,
  Friend of Genius, Learning, Art,
  Honest friend of honest heart;
Source of social elevation,
 Schemes of wide benevolence,
Pioneer to every nation,
 Up the steeps of Providence!

"Glorious records of duration!
 Sons of Genius—what a roll!
Nature's noblest illustration
 That the nations have a soul.
  Young, triumphant in the West,
  Rules her Daughter—"to be blest"—
  Wider prospect, strong and free,
  Wooing from Futurity;
England too, and yet another,
 Treasuring happier leaves of Time,
Wise and virtuous, like her mother,
 She may seize a Goal sublime.

"Not the clouds of life can smother,
 Not the frowns of Fate depress,
Saxon with a Saxon brother,
 Call'd to paths of Happiness.
  Lo! they walk the Valleys free,
  Cleave the mountain, tame the sea,
  Leave, when life below is done,
  Cities gleaming in the sun.

Noble Workers, work together;
  Shape the world for Peace to reign;
Plough the Prairie, clear the Heather,
  Bring the Golden Age again!"

X.

Near the Mansion, EDWIN speeding,
  Crossed the roofless threshing-floor;
Passed an ambulance, unheeding,
  Met Ozala at the door.
    "Why, Ozala, why away,
    From the field of strife to-day?
    Hark!—The battle shakes the air!
    William wants Ozala there!"
Spoke the Indian then sedately;
  "Peace! within thy brother lies!
Wounds—his wounds all bleeding lately,
  Mists—death-mists before his eyes!

"Onward cheering, tall and stately,
  Foremost till I saw him fall,
And the heroes charged us straitly:
  "Bear him safe to MARSTON Hall!"
    From the shrieking, from the storm,
    Soft I bore his bleeding form;
    Thrice the sun had fill'd the West,
    Ere my EAGLE reached his nest.
Wait!—IDOTHEA bending o'er him,
  Lotions soothing, cool applies;
And new victories rise before him,
  And new lustre lights his eyes."

XI.

See within, the loveliest daughters
  Of the Vale at MARSTON Hall;
See the gleam of neighboring waters,
  Dancing on the pictured wall.
    Silence there, profound, intense,
    Save the panting of suspense,
    Save the murmurs of the stream,
    Borne like music in a dream.
See a stately form reclining
  On a Sofa far within;
Thither every eye is shining,
  Speak?—To speak would seem a sin:

For expressions, intertwining,
  On that lip, and cheek and brow,
Pass in lines and hues defining,
  Now a pang, a rapture now.
    Round that manly breast and side,
    Tore the missile deep and wide;
    There a red and livid gash,
    Binds him like a fiery sash.
In that gleam of waters heaving,
  Thrown upon the pictured wall,
Moves a soft, white hand deceiving
  Missile, agony, and pall.

Soon the livid hue is leaving,
  As the closing wounds unite;
Some mysterious power reprieving,
  Changes anguish to delight.
    "Gone," he murmurs, "pain and wrack;
    Tides of life are flowing back,

With an angel bending o'er me:
With the peace of Home before me."
Then a gesture, ill agreeing
With his wild disorder'd hair;
Then convulsion quickly fleeing,
Then the shading of a care.

"Wisdom such in such a being,
Young and so unearthly fair;
Who can gaze, yet fail of seeing
Something more than human there?"
Musing thus in voiceless bliss,
Striving once her hand to kiss:
Strove his happiness to tell;
At her feet in worship fell.
Back with speed Ozala bore him,
At a sign IDOTHEA gave;
And again the sunbeam o'er him
Shimmers as the waters wave.

XII.

Joy educed from transient terror,
MARSTON'S silence quite subdued,
And with sacred sense of error,
Broken voice and word ensued:
"If, IDOTHEA, if too long,
I have wrought thee silent wrong,
Prized thy tender zeal amiss,
I am undeceived in this.
Rude revolt, and foul sedition,
Seem'd a Nemesis malign,
And thy sprightlier mind's attrition,
Wrought unwonted hate in mine.

"I had sworn, when fierce ignition
  Fired the lawless minds of men,
That this frantic coalition,
  Might extinguish it again;
    That no drop of son or sire
    I would waste on such a fire;
    Nor from me applause or cheer,
    Should this land of madmen hear.
Thus I swore; and unmolested,
  Here in peace we watch'd the war,
And the battles I detested
  Echoed only from afar.

"Once I heard a voice that jested
  With my sons o'er field and fight,
And I said, "The fiends have wrested
  Into wrong a father's right."
    Not the voice of Freedom, Fame,
    Though there be no mightier name,
    Sent my Spartan to the field,
    Brought him home upon his shield,—
Madmen fields of blood could render
  Starr'd with Delphic prophecies,
Light our mountain tops with splendor,
  Vales with anniversaries,

"All his summer surface tender,
  Rounding with their plastic hand,
Till he deem'd himself Defender,
  Egemon of Spartan land.
    But I see THOU hast a sway
    O'er the 'ills of human clay;
    Power to cure what others kill;
    Vein the blood which others spill;

And thy mission must be holy;
    E'en thy fancies seem divine;
Silent months of melancholy
    Cease to gnaw this heart of mine."

XII.

Marston Hall is silent, lonely,—
    Two—the joyful two, withdrawn,—
WILLIAM mates with EDWIN only;
    Walks the meadows, walks the lawn.
        " Who were those mysterious TWO?
        Tell me, EDWIN, tell me true!
        One too wise to be a boy;
        One a dream of light and joy:
He a youth I heard you mention
    Oft at Sydney, years ago;
She, some God's sublime intention,—
    Human bliss, or human woe?"

" In the field of mad contention,
    Thousands meet in deadly strife;
Engines fierce, of dire invention,
    Tore the sacred fanes of life;
        There upon the sanguine plain,
        Seeking still his lost ELAINE,
        Strayed a Youth, unconscious where,
        Reckless in his mute despair.
Host retiring, host assailing,
    Terror here, confusion there,
While the missiles shrieking, wailing,
    Hurtle through the darkened air.

"Fondly in his heart detailing
 Tender vows of moons ago,
Gray with sorrows unavailing,
 Passed Erasmus, sad and slow.
  Shrilling just before his brow,
  As his lips renew the vow,
  Flies a flaming shell amain.
  Bursting on the gory plain.
And from far I see him reeling,
 Backward on the dusty field ;
Rush I then with fellow-feeling,
 Aid or sympathy to yield.

"Swift away, amid the pealing,
 From the field I bear my friend ;
In a deep ravine concealing,
 Where the foe may not offend.
  O'er his breast and head I bow :
  Not a wound on face or brow !
  Yet insensible he lies ;
  Peaceful Death upon his eyes.
In his breast no throb was heaving,
 From his lips no breath of air ;
Brow and face the gloom was leaving,
 Rosy smiles returning there !

XIV.

"Wandering near this spot secluded,
 Hasten'd Roy of Marston Hall :
O'er the lifeless form I brooded ;
 Startling came the friendly call :—
  "Bring him straight to Marston Hall :
  He must have the care of all."

"Soft we bear the sunken form,
  Far from battle and the storm;
There the tender bending o'er him,
  Lotions pungent, fresh apply;
Senseless of the tears before him,
  Still no lustre lights his eye.

XV.

"Came the kindest, loveliest daughters
  Of the Vale to Marston Hall;
And the gleam of neighboring waters,
  Dances on the pictured wall.
    There is silence deep, intense,
    Save the breathing of suspense,
    Save the murmuring of the stream,
    Heard like music in a dream.
There they place my friend, reclining,
  On a Sofa far within;
Thither every eye is shining,
  But to speak would seem a sin.

"Sweet expressions, intertwining,
  O'er that lip, and cheek, and brow,
Pass in lines and hues defining,
  Now a hope, a rapture now.
    No contusion could we trace,
    O'er that sunken head and face;
    Yet the breath, the pulse no more,
    Might the skill of man restore.
Through the gleam of waters heaving,
  Thrown upon the pictured wall,
Moves a shadowy hand deceiving,
  Envious step of pain or pall.

"Smile, illusion never leaving,
　Where the moveless lids unite;
Some mysterious power reprieving,
　Clothes the brow of Death with light.
　　　Now one tint of pale distress
　　　Blends with hues of happiness;
　　　Soon dispersed, leaves no alloy,
　　　Lost in lineaments of joy.
But the trace of breezes fleeting,
　Tangles his disorder'd hair,
Ripples of the wavelets meeting,
　Intertwined and nestled there!

XVI.

"Thus he lay. Nine days retiring,
　Each had chased some hope away;
No response to our desiring;
　Yet no token of decay.
　　　Then we reason'd, day and night,—
　　　Tears between us and the light,—
　　　Can a sinless frame decay?
　　　Can the Holy mold away?
If to Marston Vault we bore him,
　Hands with reverent care composed,
If with coffin open o'er him,
　Vault and coffin left unclosed?

"There, the light of morn before him,
　Unconfined by bolt or lid,
Should the breath of heaven restore him,
　Naught would hinder, naught forbid.
　　　Thus resolved, we gently lay
　　　In his shroud the sacred clay,

And sweet odors o'er him shed,
  Reverent tears upon his head.
And we bear the bier before us,
  Down the long and flowery lane;
Knell nor requiem sounding o'er us:
  But he had a "mourning train."

"For, the roar of battle tore us,
  Echoing through the hills again,
And our bleeding fancy bore us,
  O'er another gory plain.
    O, my country! fields of strife
    Desecrate the boon of life!
    Glory woos the brave in vain,
    And Oblivion guards the slain.
Pride of battle! false, illusive;
  Who, hath found true glory there?
Who the barbarous chief obtrusive
  Made it glory thus to dare?

"But, we near the hill confusive,
  Cross the water, climb the steep;
Reach the Vault with step conclusive,
  Where the loved of ages sleep.
    Then the iron doors unclose.
    Lo, the dead disposed in rows!
    And we set our burden there.
    Near a Beauty, wondrous fair!
And her coffin, too, was open,
  Plain, unlidded, like our own,
Standing there, securely slopen,
  Resting on the wall of stone.

XVII.

"Oh! the Lovely! Is it Heaven?
　Is it Nature, makes the Fair?
Do the holy, happy Seven,
　　Rivalries of art compare?
　　　　There she smiles. We gaze in bliss;
　　　　Hope to see no face but this,
　　　　Not of death a stain, a sign:
　　　　Life is human, Death divine!
Still from charms delusive weaning,
　Show us charms beyond the veil!
There in forms divine convening
　Hues of life that never fail!

" Then we set our burden, leaning,
　Slightly touched the Lady's biere;
Lo! her brow assumes a meaning,
　Lo! the rosy smiles appear!
　　　　Then a snowy whiteness came
　　　　O'er two brows, in hue the same;
　　　　And another flush ensues,
　　　　Mutual interchange of hues;
And a dimness came, surrounding
　Hill, and Vault, and faces there;
Soft, ethereal tones were sounding
　Far above us, in the air!

" Words distinct, responsive, bounding,
　Sweet—too sweet for human thought,
Wondrous harmonies compounding,
　Wisdom, Love, and Hope, enwrought.
　　　　Then within two coffins came
　　　　Two young doves, of hue the same,

Sat upon two bosoms white,
And the bosoms heaved with light ;
And upon the eyelids, moving,
On those lips, now ruby hue,
Fell a lustre unreproving,
Fell a drop of living dew !

" And each ashy line ungrooving,
Swells into a rosy bloom,
Light of youth and love behooving,
Beauty rising from the tomb !
From the coffins both withdrew,
Walk'd the Dædal earth anew,
Gazing each with loving eyes,
Lost in questions and replies.
And with tones subdued and holy :
" We shall see them all again !"
" Arrionel, be meek and lowly ;
Thou hast sought me not in vain."

" Dreams are these ?—illusions wholly ?
Where bright Home thy gleaming gems ?
Lo ! our visions vanish slowly,
Fleeting, fading paradems !
Could it be a passing dream ?
Did I find thee by the stream ?
Stream of Nectar, at thy feet,
Rippling, murmuring slow and sweet ?
See ! Aerial birds descending,
Warbling o'er thee, lead the way !
See ! the leaping lambs attending,
Crowd along thy steps, and play !"

" Nay ;—It is the Life unending :
　　Visions only seem to be,—
　Spirit, Wisdom, Nature blending,
　　　Countless worlds invite the free !
　　　　　Hark !—be holy, and be wise !
　　　　　Life endures, and we must rise ;
　　　　　Rising, Oh ! what shall we see,
　　　　　If this Life immortal be ?
　Brighter mansions dim the former,
　　While the POSSIBLE we soar ;
　Soaring, still in Worship warmer,
　　Will He say, "I give no more?'"

IDOTHEA III.

YONDER!

OR THE

BEAUTY OF HOLINESS.

EPIDOS II.—AT HOME AGAIN.

EPISODE II.—ANALYSIS.

Joyful Meeting.—Exchange of Thought.—Progress of Soul.—Ancient Simplicity.—Revelations of Death.—Reveals not all.—Spiritual Economy.—Regions of Happier Spirits.—Wider Dominion over Matter.—Astral Life.—Improvements,—Duration,—Perpetual Peace,—Effects.—Religion,—Man, bold, presumptuous, wicked,—Lost Power over Nature.—Orson, Edwin appear.—Transmigration,—Bitter Rebuke,—Forgiveness;—Spontaneous Combustion,—Rescue,—Repentance.

YONDER!

Epidos II.—At Home Again.

I.

"Say not Fate is unrelenting,
   Mercy smiles in Nature still :
Arrimanes yields, repenting,
   Kneeling to the Holy Will.
      How the mountains smile again !
      Fragrance laughs along the plain ;
      Whispering breezes winged with light,
      Speak of peace and joy to-night.
Stars, kind stars, so sweetly shining
   In the holy depths of space,
Send their twinkling beams, entwining
   Round the sorrows of my face.

"Cease, fond heart, your long repining !
   Bliss once more is on the earth ;
Joyful spirits, close inclining,
   Hold a festival of mirth :
      Sweet compassion, power divine,
      Smooths the azure hyalline ;

Cherub happiness comes down,
　Through the cloudlets golden-brown!
Through each soul the Beauty streaming,
　Thanks and adoration swell;
This old heart, with raptures teeming,
　Must its tale of rapture tell.

"I had lost the heavenly seeming,
　Lonely lost in wintry years;
Lo! again the world is beaming
　With the banishment of tears!
　　Lonely I shall feel no more;
　　Angels smile within my door!
　　All the love of life I find,
　　Flowing back in whispers kind.
Heaven hath brought my darling treasure,
　Blooming to my arms again,—
Light of age, and bliss of leisure,
　With his lovely, lost Elaine!

"Call not mine a human measure:
　Call not mine a mingled lot;
Life is made of pain and pleasure,
　But MY pain is all forgot.
　　O, my joy must be restrained;
　　Joy for him, my son, regained!
　　I return within my door,
　　See him, hear him, as of yore!
Ah! too oft a glance invidious
　Drops from some malignant star;
Here, e'en here, may powers insidious,
　Steal around our bliss to mar."

II.

"Marked ye not the meteor gliding,
    Like a spirit o'er the rill,
While the lamps Titanian chiding,
    Leaped to catch it on the hill?
        Beauteous night of moon and star.
        How I think of nights afar,
        When, dear father, you and I
        Looked upon the Summer sky!
Oh! my heart was half persuaded,
    Bliss is more than Earth can show;
Angel-glory, faintly shaded,
    In these elements below.

"Half my blooming hopes have faded,
    Hopes the True, the Good to see;
Now the worlds are all pervaded
    With a Holiness to me.
        Now a purity divine
        Robes the shining Crystalline:
        Now I know the grades and graces
        Crowning those eternal spaces.
Such the Patriarchal ages,
    Simple, tranquil, wise, sincere,
Loving souls and leading sages,
    These to rule and those revere.

"Those to fill the Sacred pages,
    Those to seek the Good, the True;
Kindness, care, the people's wages,
    Love and trust the Sage's due.
        Such abodes of humble worth
        Angels visit here on earth,

And a Beauty dwells below,
   More than Wisdom, Truth can show:—
Pity for the pang distressing,
   Mercy for the erring poor,
For the meek in heart, a blessing,
   For the fatherless, a door.

" We are Christians, sin-confessing,
   Fighting for the Faith divine;
Blind apostasies repressing,
   Wrangling branches of the Vine.
      We revere the rights of man,
      But we hate the Puritan,
      Keep the Constitution pure,
      If it make our wealth secure.
Ah! the heretic, the tory,
   How they rend the hallowed Fane!
Never down the steeps of story,
   Shall its lustre shine again!

III.

" Here, within a world of Duty,
   Needful rights and claims abound,
Shining through a veil of Beauty,
   Shadows of the more profound;
      Twilight of the perfect Day,
      Gone, or coming far away;
      Echoes from a distant shore,
      Bright Evangels coming o'er;
And with awe our hearts can feel it,
   Admiration leans to hear,
Saying, 'Death will not reveal it,
   Yonder, Light will re-appear.'

" Ah! this clay cannot conceal it;
  Death will not reveal it all;
  Broken seals will not unseal it.
    Though the Galaxies may fall.
      Truth is but the dawn we see,
      Twilight of Eternity;
      Wing to Orbits viewless here,
      Twilight only can appear:
    Brighter as the soul advances,
      Yet the Central Flame unseen,
    And the loftiest Orb that dances,
      Sees but Orbs that intervene.

" Ray descends, and lightning glances,
    Kindling from the Source Divine,
  Beauty charms and Truth entrances,
    But they all in visions shine.
      This is all that worlds may be,
      All material eyes can see;
      Where the intellectual ray
      Must be limited by clay.
    Where the immaterial eye,
      Disembodied, yet defined,
    May rejoice in space forever.
      Self in one self-conscious mind.

" Wants material, prompt endeavor.
    In the other worlds as here;
  There the vile and virtuous sever,
    These to hope, and those to fear:
      There desires imperious swell,
      There beliefs, affections dwell,
      Pleasures of voluptuous mind,
      Wants to crave, and loves to bind;

Vain pursuit, and brief fruition,
  There allure, and there delude ;
Each a limited condition,
  Acting through Infinitude.

IV.

"There to regions bright, ideal,
  Fancy soars aloft to find,
Charms created from the real,
  Purer joys for heart and mind.
    There the Muse in Epic shade,
    Draws the manners ere they fade,
    Draws the present and the past,
    Draws the Beautiful, the Vast:
And, to loftier views inspiring,
  Woos Improvement o'er the clime,
While the world, aroused, admiring,
  Springs to aims and arts sublime.

"Then to classic Halls retiring,
  Science, Truth, Philosophy,
Mold the ardent mind, enquiring
  For the triumphs yet to be.
    Reason soars from sphere to sphere.
    Whispers all she whispers here ;
    Whispers more, the more sublime,
    Worlds of space and worlds of time :
Nature's genial inspiration,
  Kindling all the sons of light ;
Freedom, Virtue, Emulation,
  Consecrate the Rule of Right.

" Last, amid the orbs' ovation,
   Steals a whisper from the Deep.
 And the Prophet's proclamation
   Thunders from the cloudy steep:
       'Life, immortal life is thine;
       Right is sacred, Truth divine:
       But the Holy One am I,
       And the Holy is the High;
 Lo! the Schechinah abideth,
   Clouded o'er the Mercy Seat;
 Where the Holy One resideth,
   Judgment, Truth, and Mercy meet.

" There no craving want collideth,
   When the righteous deed is done.
 Holy Dignity decideth,
   And the angel is begun.
       Not for terrors or distress,
       Not for views of happiness;
       If the Holy be to gain,
       Charity and Mercy vain.
 Here is Beauty, pure, unfading,
   Parts conspiring for the whole;
 For the ear the stock, the blading,
   All of Nature for the Soul.

" And the holy angels aiding,
   Bring the Soul from sphere to sphere,
 Many mansions, graded, grading,
   Till the dust with Soul appear.
       Matter working all for this,
       Wings the grain of dust to bliss,
       God's creative hand unseen,
       Molding in the worlds between:

6

While rich harmonies are flowing,
   Through the echoing mansions sent,
As the Good redeemed are going
   Up from bale and banishment."

V.

"I came near, the bliss to enter,
   Climes of perfect Purity,
Glorious mansion, near the centre,
   But, one taint they found in me:
      In my soul a deep regret,—
      Love I could not soon forget:
      Far, my heart was far away.
      In the walks of Solar day:
And sweet images obtruded,
   Lowing herd and cottage white,—
One despairing face, secluded,
   Ever pleading in my sight.

"Fondly o'er the past I brooded,
   Sought the lonely mountain side,
E'en dear mother's arms eluded,
   Warmer now than when she died!
      Then she told me I could go,
      Could resume my life below,
      If I would endure the pain,
      There to live and die again:
That my virgin clay untainted,
   In the Vault could not decay;
Canonized by love, and sainted,
   Dust would not resolve away.

"Then her beauteous world she painted,
   How she found a mansion there,
Made me with the Blest acquainted,
   O, the lovely! O, the fair!
      There, they said my name should be,
      THEA of FIDELITY;
      But IDOTHEA down below,
      In the world I wished to go.
      Then they taught me mystic skill,
      Strange activities of Will;
      Atoms of the living frame,
      Subject all to Mind became:
      Molecules move at my command,
      As you move the arm or hand!
Tutor'd thus, I soon could hide me,
   Viewless in the viewless air;
Not the keenest eye beside me,
   Would detect my presence there.

VI.

"Mite from atomite compelling,
   I can float upon the ray,
Make my temporary dwelling,
   Folded in the beam of day;
      Mid the glory of the sheen,
      Strike my harp, and sing unseen,
      And the voice shall seem to be
      Music in your memory.
Loftier minds, with powers imperial,
   Sway these particles with ease;
Rule the bonds of form material,
   Shaping, moulding as they please.

Holy Essence, pure, ethereal,
   Rising through successive spheres.
Moves along the clouds aerial,
   Void of sin and guilty fears.
      Yet within their essence fine,
      Limited by power divine,
      Forms material clothe them still,
      Subject to the higher Will,
Till within the One Volition,
   Spirit unalloy'd and free,
Spirit reigns o'er all condition,
   Molding this Immensity.

VII.

"There, in pure Autonomy,
   Personal, eternal Right,
Sums the bright Economy,
   Source of all within the light.
      There, the Holy is the True,
      Spirit, making One of two,
      Fountain of the Good, the Fair,
      Spirit here, and Nature there;
Rivers from the True, the Holy,
   Flowing down the worlds around,
Streams of Error welling slowly
   From the darkness under-ground.

"Streams of Error, creeping lowly,
   Chill the shivering soul with night,
Ebon chain of Melancholy,
   Into blackness turns the light.
      Ah! the distant, dark degree,
      Down below the joyous free!

Here material fetters bind,
Rule, incarcerate the mind;
There the chainless powers of Soul
All her INSTRUMENTS control.
Ah! the erring heart will harden,
Walls of flesh will not obey;
Nature hath no Code for pardon;
Who will roll the stone away?

"Yonder, in the happy Garden,
Soul is queen of wall and gate;
Not the sword, and not the warden,
Bid to wave, or set to wait.
SPIRIT, queen of Beauty there,
Makes, because she loves, the fair;
Radiant forms of light and shade,
Glide along the summer glade;
Innocence, in dimples twining,
Purity in mold and hue,
Lucid ringlets, silken, shining,
Twinkling with the morning dew.

VIII.

" Evening revels, joyful voices,
Holy songs of ancient days,
Heaven consents, and man rejoices,
Where to revel is to praise.
Silence keeps her peace no more,
Strikes the prelude o'er and o'er,
Then, up springs the holy strain,
Pauses lengthen into pain.

O, I swell with sweet devotion,
  Echoing glory of the lay,
Waves of music and emotion,
  Circling o'er the hills away.

"Tears and smiles, like tides of ocean,
  Sweet, responsive, come and go;
Hopes and fears in soft commotion,
  Full of love together flow:
    With each hope, a fond caressing,
    With each fear, a kiss, a blessing;
    O, the rapture thus to meet,
    Where our parting is to greet!
Sunlit hills arose behind me,
  Pinion'd with the rays of morn,
Fragrant solitudes entwined me,
  Blushing roses newly born.

"In the void I seemed to find me,
  Borne in mother's arms again;
Joy of sweet return assigned me,—
  Rapture verges into pain!
    'I shall leave this beauteous form,
    All with life celestial warm,
    Wake the tranced dust again,
    Which they loved to call Elaine.
Let us linger, let us ponder!
  Mother, we are coming soon,
Let us go a-while to wander,
  In our paths beneath the moon.

"Friends, sweet friends, are weeping yonder:
  How soft hands will welcome give!
Not the angels here are fonder;
  There to love is still to live.

Let us go;—the beings here,
With a wonder mix a fear;
Potent, beautiful, refined,
Merging almost into mind,
Molding organs as they please,
In the clouds, amid the seas;
Verily, a timid stranger,
Move I here, although with thee;
Let me go, and be a ranger
In my dear mortality.'

IX.

" In the gloam of astral summer,
We descend, communing so:
Here again, a fond New-Comer,
Tell my tale of love below.
There, I know, will love endure;
Shall I find it here as pure?
There affections deep and warm,
Bloom and beautify the form.
There the constant, happy being
Cheers for centuries a home;
And the ages, softly fleeing,
Leave no restless wish to roam.

" Peaceful Polities agreeing,
Fruits of Industry endure.
Still the rising millions seeing,
What the ages may secure.
Worlds contiguous, rich, and fair,
Send their late Improvements there,
Art and Genius dare to soar.
Heights, abysses still for more:

We can make the needful pinion,
    Fly with thought upon the beam,
Be at will in each Dominion,
    See its new creations teem.

X.

" Noble aims by Wisdom guided,
    Sequences in causes seen,
No true blessing unprovided,
    No defeat to intervene.
        There no cruel wars annoy,
        Hand to ravage, arm destroy,
        Cycles of Improvement flow.
        Sages rule and kingdoms grow.
All contingencies provided,
    Who will dare assail the State?
Plans and policies decided,
    Ask no waste of long debate.

" Who betrays the trust confided?
    Who could wish the glory less?
Hope deferr'd is faith derided :
    To be holy is to bless.
        Streams and fountains ever pure,
        Majesty that must endure ;
        Not the splendor of an hour,—
        There Antiquity is power.
Oh! I seem'd a lost creation,
    Viewless in the blaze of day,
Overwhelm'd with revelation,
    And it hasten'd me away.

" Faith is there a demonstration,
  Beaming from the worlds around;
Worship every heart's oblation,
  And with Love the Altar crowned.
    There no Councils meet to see,
    If the Gods be one or three;
    East and West may still be one,
    Signing no Henoticon.
Who demands a Formulary?
  Nature teaches how to love,
And to love the LUMINARY,
  Is the Formula above.

" True devotion cannot vary,
  If the worship be of ONE;
Loving souls are planetary,
  And their Centre is the SUN.
    Yet the holiest there can see
    Heights of holier purity;
    Lo! to One behind the scene,
    E'en the heavens are unclean.
But He sees the good ascending
  All his holy Alps below,
Hope and Trust serene attending,
  Heights of purer bliss to know.

XI.

"Man, bold man, with impious daring,
  Frames his Ritual for the skies;
Earth's voluptuous banquets sharing,
  Heedless of the orphan's cries.
    Dares to draw the frighten'd world,
    Bleating round his flag unfurl'd:

'Lo! my banner! Sinners flee!
  Vengeance howls for all but me;'
While himself, a taper gleaming,
  In the blaze of Solar day,
Urim, Thummim, gazing, beaming,
  Shine within the Milky-Way!

"Bold, bad man, to wear the seeming;
  Impious man, to say I KNOW,
When the Thrones, in meek self-deeming,
  Pray their Primal Suns to show!
    Still the monster, sire to me,
    Spins his Sunday homily;
    Dozing hundreds, kneeling low,
    Pay to hear him say, I KNOW!
But the wandering angels know him,
  Mother, daughter, know him too;
And the Wrath to Come will show him
  What it is to mock the True.

"She, deluded, felt below him,—
  Ah! to hear her tell it all!—
Forced in shame her troth to owe him:
  Forced to silence in her fall.
    Once, within the grove we came—
    I began to learn his name,—
    At her side, I gazed to see
    What a stately man was he.
There, convulsed with some emotion,
  There she sank upon the ground;
Through her lips he poured a potion,
  And she slept a sleep profound.

"Then he seemed to seize a notion ;
  In his face, some pale alarm,
Like a burden of devotion,
  Raised her in his brawny arm,
    Bore her shrunken weight away,
    Down to where the Tannery lay ;
    Left me wailing near the tree,
    Frightened at the mystery.
In the foulest Vat he threw her,
  Vat abandoned long ago ;
Lost to all the friends that knew her,
  Lost to friends who wished to know.

XII.

"I was rescued. Heaven above us
  Listens to the orphan's cry ;
None,—if none below will love us,
  Weeping Love will leave the sky.
    I was rescued. Soft, white hands
    Found me where the Walnut stands,
    Bore me to this happy Dale,
    Gave me years of bliss for bale.
Years will bring their own fruition,
  Years will bring their sorrows too ;
I, a maid of lorn condition,
  Found one Sorrow, and it grew !

"O, how sweet the recognition !
  Yonder Orchard, Hall, I see !
Oh ! how deep the demolition !
  Oh ! the hopes that died in me !
    ORSON bore his prize away,
    Snatched from vows and vocal lay ;

Orson grasped ;—I saw his face ;
Shivered in his rude embrace;
O'er the hills in haste away,
Stones, and steeps, and mountains gray,
Poor Elaine invoking Death ;
Death obeyed, and stole her breath.
And they laid her frame unbreathing,
In the Vault, one starless night,
And the Parson, sour and seething,
Drained his Burgundy in spite."

XIII.

"See, Elaine, the PARSON lighting!
Edwin too!—They mean to call.
Fie! Erasmus,—think of fighting?
Prudence will be best for all!
Caution well becomes the young ;
Wait, and hear his oily tongue ;
Leave contingencies to me :
If you slay him, we must flee!
Shores are worn, and mountains hoven,
By the patient hand of Time ;
And the spirit's worth is proven,
As endurance grows sublime."

Full of phrases interwoven,
Entered Orson, like a beam,
All his words unbraided, cloven,
Thus prismatic of his theme.
Ah! that startling vision threw
All his white to red and blue,
And the features of Elaine
Flushed and faded, flushed again.

Stood he, blank;—nor stir, nor token
  Drew his gaze to Arrionel;
All his favorite terms unspoken:
  Skeptic, traitor, infidel!

There his Victim, fresh, unbroken,
  Sat o'erflowing with a smile,
Near the wainscot, painted, oaken,
  With a sprig of Cammomile.
    Then she drops the sprig amain,
    Smiling at the floor again,
    Rose with modest, mute delay,
    Looked at him, and looked away;
Dulcet, like a grotto streamy,
  Like a murmuring ocean-shell,
With a music, low and dreamy,
  Vanished in her Citadel.

For, Hyperion, golden, beamy,
  Through the window from the West,
Sent a column, azure, gleamy,
  Sloping to the Parson's breast.
    Out the flowing, misty beam,
    Words serene, symphonious stream,
    Came like incense on the air,
    Born afar, yet breathing there,
Words judicial, slow, emphatic,
  Holy, truthful, deferent,
Never wavering, vain, erratic,
  Caustic, cleaving as they went

XIV.

"Deem not, man of dark intention
  Virtue, honor, truth inane;

Deem not heaven a sheer invention,
  Sybil of some priestly brain!
    Deem not sacred themes, a toy,
    Fit to pander, lure, decoy;
    Toils which you may set for game,
    Nets for treasure, wealth, and fame.
When of heavenly joys debating,
  Holy men their hopes impart,
Have you found a chord vibrating
  Through the universal heart?

"You, in closets calculating,
  Think with hopes and fears to play?
Fast and Formula creating,
  Ask Credulity to pay!
    Fatal error. Faith is true;
    Holy men are sages too;
    Reverent, humble pure, sincere,
    Touching holy things with fear.
Noble souls with generous feeling,
  Call'd to spread the Food divine,
Souls that weigh the Word revealing,
  Hearts of love, and not of wine.

"Men, who taste the Pneuma stealing
  Down the paths of life below;
Men whose words the Lord is sealing,
  From the Pulpit as they flow.
    Brave, warm hearts which seek to know
    All the Lord of Light may show,—
    Nature, Science, Matter, Mind,—
    Burn no Brunos for mankind!

Liberal souls, expanding ever,
    Hearts to love, and lips to teach,
Grasping truths at each endeavor,
    Truths your soul will never reach!

"Fearless souls, who tremble never.
    When new leaves of Science turn,
When the clouds of Fate dissever,
    And we see new systems burn :
        Souls who see that Truth is God,
        In the stars, beneath the sod ;
        Give her honor, reverence due,
        Love her, just for being true.
Glad Evangels of the PATER,
    Wing'd with tidings glad to men,
You, a mouthing Imitator,
    Trampling what you fail to ken.

"You, a bold, impetuous prater,
    Odorous of the fiery still,
Dooming each to Satan's crater,
    Who presumes to have a Will.
        So your homilies be strong,
        Reckless of the right or wrong ;
        You, a perfect infidel,
        Dooming infidels to hell :
Till, in minds of calm reflection,
    Springs a doubt of Truth revealed,
And the hope of Resurrection,
    And the Life Above are sealed.

XV.

"You, the fluent, bold Deceiver,
    Found a fond, believing Fair ;

Told her, every true believer
　　Heaven assigns the Pastor's share;
　　　Told her, others all consent,
　　　Sure, the Beauty must relent;
　　　Woo'd her, won her, made her seem.
　　　Odious in her self-esteem:
Poisoned, plunged in foulest water,
　　Her, the loveliest of her race,—
　　Her, Earl Marston's beauteous daughter,
　　Lost delight of Marston Place.

XVI.

"Didst thou fly—forget the orphan,
　　Wailing by the Walnut tree?
Didst forget thy treasured morphine,
　　Dropt in haste, to poison me?
　　　Didst thou wait for years to slay?
　　　Drag thy child to death away?
　　　Lock her in the Vault to rot?
　　　Canst thou hear and see her not?
Part of thee, which is eternal,
　　Interfused with Holiness!
See the powers of Life supernal;
　　O, be wise, and learn to bless!

"Thou art wed to wants diurnal,
　　Wicked, wandering long, too long;
Far in climes forever vernal;
　　Mother loves, and love is strong.
　　　Rise, and bless thy child to-day;
　　　Life thou couldst not take away;
　　　Rise, and seize this life divine;
　　　Mother's love would make it thine;

Angels teach her how to live,—
Love, be holy, and forgive.
Oh! she bids you come and share,
Life and Love are holy there.
There the suns in glory rolling,—
Truth and Love incarnadine.
Mercy, Holiness impoling,
Give to love a joy divine."

XVII.

Lo! a flame spontaneous darted,
Fierce from Orson's mouth and ears,
Azure mists around him started.
In his eyes some fiery tears.
All, astonished, ran to save;
Vain the willing aid we gave;
Water decomposed amid
Fervent heat of brow and lid!
Oh! his moving objuration!
Oh! his yell of speechless pain!
On the ground in desolation,
Calling piteously, "Elaine!"

Leaping forth in desperation,
Orson seized his horse to go,
But the horse in consternation,
Fled far down the Vale below.
Orson, slave to wine, alas!
Long had plied his bowl and glass;
Deep excess his chief delight,
Drink and wassail late at night.
This, and o'er-excited feeling,
Fired the igneous magazine:

Nature keeps her stores for healing,
 But volcanos burn between.

To his side Idothea stealing,
 Lingered o'er his fallen frame;
Feeble rose his deep appealing,
 And his face was all in flame.
  Softly from her waist she drew
  Amianthine sheet of blue,
  Wrapped his blazing head and face,
  In its close and cool embrace.
Slow the flame, unfed, subsided,
 Smothered in its vital source,
And the spark of life, divided,
 Held within its living force.

Slow the vital powers confided,
 Stir the throbs of heart and vein,
And the wavering scale decided,
 Orson lives and breathes again.
  Changed!—a joy, a wonder wrought,
  Changed in hue of feeling, thought,
  Morbid wants consumed away,
  Smiling like a child he lay;
With a docile heart to ponder
 O'er the possible, the true,
Hoping here, and gazing yonder,
 With a life Divine in view.

XVIII.

Now he saw a wondrous beauty
 O'er the Vale, the Mountain flow;

Flowers along the path of duty,
   And a burning thirst, TO KNOW.
      In his soul a sweet resolve,
      Whispers, as his thoughts revolve,
      And a feeling from above,
      Comes incumbent, like a dove.
Flies his life-long cloud of sadness,
   Not indulgence could dispel,
And a strange, romantic gladness
   Comes among his thoughts to dwell.

" Blest Elaine!—forgive my badness?
   Angel! how couldst thou forgive!
Fiend was I, a monster Madness,
   Couldst thou wish to see ME live!
      Didst thou say, thy mother loves,
      Loves the fiend who slays the doves!
      Didst thou say, I might again
      See the angel I had slain!
Worlds of God! reveal your wonders!
   I will wander, toil, explore;
I will cleave the cloud that sunders
   Soul from heights the wise adore;

" I will brave the mountain thunders.
   They are God's behest, I know,
Wreak my soul for wicked blunders,
   Pile my penalties of woe.
      Teaching?—what have I to teach?
      Tides and tempests, ye must preach!
      Something holy, something true,
      Come, and dress my soul anew!
Pangs of Death! be harsh, unsparing;
   Seen have I HER agony!

Pity none of Nature sharing,
  She hath borne it all for me!

"Wave, and wind, and waters daring,
  Age shall win the prize of youth;
Far, to classic shores repairing,
  Drink at all the wells of Truth.
    Rise through plains of Power divine,
    Plains where Beauty, Wisdom shine,
    Pass the azure, moral zone,
    Justice, Virtue, throne on throne,
Reach the Holy Land of Beulah,—
Life, this worthless life, a-wane,—
Might this toil retrieve my Lulah!
Might this end repay Elaine!"

IDOTHEA III.

YONDER!

OR THE

BEAUTY OF HOLINESS.

EPIDOS III.—URANONDE.

EPIDOS III.—ANALYSIS.

Home, Natural Sympathies, Associations.—Virginia, Traditions, Memorials.—Our Country, Scenery, History, Prospects.—Trisagion.—This Habitable World, New Applications of Natural Law, Art, Science of the Future, Powers of Man.—Morning of the Nuptials, The Wedding, The Convocation.—Nymphagion.

YONDER!

Epidos III.—Uranonde.

I.

"Home, Elysian Home! up yonder,
   There I found my lost Elaine;
Blissful there to live and wander;
   Here is bliss, Old Home! again.
      There I saw the Spring unfold
      Amaranths of shining gold,
      Heard melodious waters flow
      O'er the pebbles white as snow:
Rode the flashing waves of Ocean,
   Play'd with Nereids of the Deep,
THEA steering clouds in motion,
   While I met her on the steep.

"Then we passed, with mute devotion,
   Down Amola dales to roam,
Muse, and point, in wrapt emotion,
   Far away to 'Old Sweet Home!'
      Humble home, forever dear!
      We, your children, greet thee here,
      Pass'd, repass'd the dim abyss;
      Left our glorious home for this!

Gone, ye tones, that love expresses,
    When the mother lulls the child!
Far away the golden tresses
    Showed upon me, when she smiled!

" Fragrant memories! Sweet caresses!
    Come around this throb of pain!
Fathers lead :—the mother blesses :
    Holy blessings, come again!
        In yon world I found awhile
        Once again a mother's smile,
        Found her by the emerald Sea.
        Her who nursed my infancy :
Left her in a shining mansion,
    Blooming health and youth again!
Looking o'er the blue Expansion,—
    She and Lulah, by the Main.

II.

" Is not Home a sweet creation?
    Balmy Love has nestled there :
Nature's dear elimination
    From a Universe of care?
        Lo! a mother's hand was here,
        Leaving long memorials dear,
        Leaving memories, clustered round
        Wall and window, garden, ground.·
Hail, thou blissful, humble dwelling!
    When I see thy walls afar,
In my heart a NAME comes, swelling,
    And I turn to yonder star!

"And my tedious tongue keeps telling
　　Vanish'd joys, that never stay;
Like a spring, forever welling
　　In the listening light of day.
　　　　Sweet IDOTHEA, we were blest,
　　　　In these mountains of the West;
　　　　Father, mother, daughters, sons,
　　　　Toiling, free, contented ones.
Mountain Home! nor rich, nor showy;
　　Ours a heritage of love;
New delights, when hot, when snowy;
　　Now, IDOTHEA from above!

"Lovely lands have had their Chloe,
　　Holy lands have had their Ruth,
Born for thee, Assarigoa,
　　Bright IDOTHEA brings her truth.
　　　　Yes, my Country, fair and free;
　　　　Beauteous land from sea to sea,
　　　　Let us not the planets roam,
　　　　If we find in thee a home!
See! the star of dawn is rising
　　O'er yon misty mountain now;
All the landscape courts surmising,—
　　Is it Terra's—Saturn's brow?

"Wandering Spirits, not advising,
　　Take these Vales for Vales above;
Lands most genial climes comprising,
　　Scenes to claim an angel's love:
　　　　Vast Atlantis, beauteous, blest,
　　　　Rising, rolling, East and West;
　　　　Tent celestial arching o'er
　　　　Mountain, Prairie, Ocean, Shore:

9

Once the Indian's empyrean ;—
   Wigwams on the mountain side,
Hailed their wild ANDANUKEYAN,
   O'er the woodlands, far and wide.

"And all night, on hills KADEAN,
   Brightly blazed the Council-Fire,
Painted warriors, Cyclopean,
   Rang the yell of fierce desire.
      Gone, the maid, the lover too ;
      Gone, the shining stone Canoe ;
      Both have left the land of snows ;
      O'er their bones the ploughman goes.
Strange successors claim the Highland,
   Strange adventurers crowd the Shore,
While afar, the Summer Island,
   Looms mysterious, as before.

III.

" Vales and woodlands consecrated !
   Holy voices fill ye now ;
Genius, Art, Devotion mated,
   Tread the mead, the mountain brow :
      Hand to build, and axe to cleave ;
      Anthems pealing, morn and eve,
      Thou no more a land of snow,—
      Temples rise and cities grow.
Oh ! my Country ! crown the story !
   Make the nations pause to hear ;
Lo ! the Orient, grave and hoary,
   Looks, and lends a docile ear !

"Be the record of thy glory,
  'Friend of Art, and foe of Arms!'
First to sweep the banner gory,
  From the heraldry of Charms.
    Thou hast fought, and bled, and won;
    Thou hast had a Washington;
    Is it infamy to rise,
    Rule the storm, assert the skies?

"First in War!"—sublime induction!
  Crown the Cromlecs, heap the stones!
Prove your engines of destruction,
  Pile your pyramids of bones!

"Yawning jaws are made for suction;
  Let the ocean spawn flow in!
What's absorption,—what eruction?
  Is the taste of blood a sin?
    Nay, Columbia! impious strife
    Dares invade immortal life!
    Soils the holiness of sense!
    Mocks the laws of Providence!
Thine the hour,—the last position;
  Thine to sublimate a Race!
Spurn the shackles of tradition!
  Seize thy heaven-appointed place!

"God hath given the high commission;
  Thou art fond of power and fame;
Make the stars an exhibition,
  What the Race of man became!
    Not to ravage, not to slay,
    Not to shame the light of day,
    Not, one score of years, create,
    Next, destroy and desolate!

Put thy hand upon the billow;
  Bid the troubled sea be still;
Make the golden cloud thy pillow;
  Lo! the lightnings bow to Will!

"Take thy harp from off the willow,—
  Man's captivity is o'er!—
Like the crawling armadillo,
  Roving armies leave the shore.
    Weave for kings the purple robe;
    Strew thy riches o'er the globe;
    For the homeless find a door,
    Clothe the naked, feed the poor;
At the helm of State, Aurelian,
  Cincinnatus at the plough,
Solon at the perihelion,
  Beauty, Virtue, Freedom—Thou!

IV.

"Hail, Columbia! rise to glory!
  But the glory must be pure;
Light the nations with your story,
  Something bright that shall endure.
    Flowers of Eden, spring again,
    O'er the Idumæan plain;
    Dire Armadas fright no more
    Barbarous tribe, or desert shore.
Let thy great SAGENE, entwining
  Ind, Cathay, Arabia, draw
Distant nations,—long declining,—
  Under Nature's holy law.

"Here, elate and unrepining,
    Wanderers of the world may roam,
Kindred, native land, resigning,
    Find in thee a welcome home.
        O'er each blooming land shall shine,
        Smile for smile, her sons and thine,
        Tears of mutual Friendship flow,
        When they meet, and when they go;
Holy vows and views congenial,
    Hearts of distant climes unite,
Errors weak, offences venial,
    Pardoned ere the fall of night.

"Land of promise! mean or menial
    Deem the toiler's hard renown?
Count the mines of wealth perennial,
    Waiting to be wafted down!
        Rear the Fane, enlarge the Mart,
        Grace the shore with shrines of Art;
        Shining rivers vie to be
        Menials for the sovran sea!
Fluent tongues are in the distance,
    Lisping through the gates of morn;
Sages, moulding for existence,
    Poets, waiting to be born.

"Purge away each dull resistance,
    Lend the conscious ear to hear,
Rising up the steep Plenistence,
    All the Infinite so near!
        Dust of monarchs, kings unknown,
        Mingled, moulded with thy own;
        Breathing, living souls above,
        Mirror'd in the dust we love!

Hold the urn, immortal Mother!
  We have sacred dust for thee;
From this Home we seek another;
  Keep Idothea's dust for me!

V.

"Father, see!—the morning blushes;
  See, Elaine! the summit gray!
Oh! the beauteous, rosy flushes,
  Rising from the realms of day!
    Still the stars, like shimmering steel,
    Keen and twinkling, seem to reel,
    Down along the Orient sky,
    In the laughing light they fly!
All among those gleaming Islands,
  Dancing in the Deep divine,
Angels, on their summer Highlands,
  Seize their harps, and take the sign.

"Emerald seas, and azure Skylands,
  Ring the Orisons of love:
Sounding Orient, echoing Vilands,
  Crown, the choruses above.
    Come, Elaine,—Idothea, bring
    Harp and heart:—The earth must sing!
    Heaven is here, and yonder light
    Comes to fill immortal sight!
Take thy Harp from out the Silence,
  Lift thy heart above the Seen;
Sounding chords, in holy Trilence,
  May unfold the light between.

VI.

TRISAGION.

I. 1.

Deem not, men of cumbrous clay!
  Men of clay alone can think,—
  Wreathe the chain of golden link,
Feel the Impulse far away.
Oh! the living, bounding Essence
Fills the morning's erubescence!
In the stars the Glory lives,
And the joy which glory gives.
SPIRIT there in sweet delay,
Sparkles through celestial clay;
There warm bosoms learn to know
Pulse of joy and pulse of woe.

I. 2.

FOUNTAIN of the viewless deep,
  Send the sacred gush around,
  Breathe the universal sound,
Rippling waves that never sleep!
Bounteous SPIRIT, warm the skies!
O'er the rolling planets rise!
Mid the restless worlds divine,
Let no slumbering soul decline!
Give the wandering winds a power;
Voices put in leaf and flower;
Give the duteous Stars delight
In the bliss of doing right!

I. 3.

Hopes instinctive, swell, inspire,
  Sinless, stainless, undefined,
  In all worlds that hold a Mind,
In all minds that feel desire.
HOLY SPIRIT, these are thine;
Thou art in the suns that shine;
Warming, kindling, whispering sweet,
Thou art in the hearts that beat.
Thus to feel our essence glow,
This is bliss, above, below.
Hope, is high and Life is free,
Dust must draw its joy from thee.

II. 1.

Boundless, bright magnificence,
  Rolling round immensity,
  Countless worlds in spaces free,
Shining with Benevolence!
Glorious Highways, range on range,
Beautiful, effulgent, strange!
Labyrinthine paths entwine,
Winding to the INNER SHRINE.
Ocean tides of golden light,
Flowing o'er primeval Night!
What may urge ye, what may draw,
Word, or Wisdom, Power, or Law?

II. 2.

Gazing Science spreads her wing;
  Truth invokes the kindling mind;
  Genius finds, and burns to find;
Where the supermundane Spring?

Where the nameless Power that dwells
In the everlasting wells?
Minds of high, celestial range,
Mount the wildering paths of change,
Watch the Wonders, as they go,
Forming, form'd, above, below;
Fold their weary wings, and wait.
Trembling at the golden Gate.

II. 3.

Hail, bright forms of Entity!
  Science soaring mid the Night.
  Truth emerges, robed in white.
Science, Wisdom! What are ye?
Holy Essences sublime,
Dropt within the realms of time?
Sent around to make us know
Something whiter than the snow,
Something purer than the tear,
Dropt upon the maiden's bier;
Something Holy in the Word,
In the Voice that Moses heard?

III. 1.

Vaulted worlds of space and time!
  Thoughts within, and thoughts around,
  Are ye bounded, or unbound?
By this mystery sublime?
Finite things must have a sum:
Things must end, as things become;
Wing away beyond the ALL.
Bounded space, or bounding Wall.

Who can comprehend the Vast?
Who can soar and see the Last?
Where the Rock that must sustain?
Where the adamantine chain?

III. 2.

POWER SUPREME! thy Word sustains;
  Subject suns in reverence roll,
  Feel invisible control.
Need no adamantine chains!
Worlds of beauty, suns of power.
Draw from thee their natal hour,
Thee, Omnipotent to sway;
At thy frown they flee away,
And the bounded mind can see
Suns and systems as they flee:
Voices sweet of Power Supreme,
Whispering in the passing beam.

III. 3.

Justice, Mercy, Truth divine,
  Rise to HOLINESS in thee,
  Absolute in Purity,
Mystery forever thine.
Mystery, forever free;
Suns and systems sing of thee.
Work thy Will, below, above;
Law! but not the law of Love.
We are GREATER than the sun,
We can call thee, "Holy One!"
Here, my spirit pours to thee,
Morning strains of Ecstasy.

VII.

" Priest, and prince, and Elevator,
  Working for the time to be ;
Working for the great Creator,
  Man will rise to Liberty.
    Lead, my Country! and with thee,
    Savage lands will haste to be ;
    Nations rise, and see the day ;
    Chains of Nature fall away.
Earth is old, but must grow older,
  Beautiful in hill and dale ;
Beautiful for each beholder :—
  Spirits ride upon the gale.

" Pierce the hills with engines bolder,
  Fell the forest, drain the marsh ;
Shade the hot, defend the colder,
  Turn to garden spots the harsh.
    Man shall moderate the storm,
    Change his icy hills to warm ;
    Wisdom, patience, courage, toil,
    Make of barren sands a soil.
Half the lands are yet in fallow,
  And the hungry cry for bread ;
Young the race, and mostly shallow,
  Hard of heart, and hot of head.

" Worn with rheums, with visage sallow,
  Dwelling in the stagnant fen ;
Left to weeds and useless mallow,
  Spots that should be homes for men.
    Earth and Ocean must endure,
    Till the race shall be mature :

Soul replaced by loftier soul,
　　While the ripening ages roll.
Man shall vindicate his Maker,
　　Make the round green earth a charm ;
If not leader, overtaker,
　　If not glory, not alarm.

VIII.

"Rise in beauty, toiling nations!
　　Angels keep the record fair ;
Fill the light with revelations,
　　Regions beaming in the air !
　　　　Hark ! the ever-breathing voice
　　　　Of the Olams cries, rejoice !
　　　　Nature holds her hand to me ;
　　　　Glories in the lines I see!
Earth's volcanic powers relenting,
　　Heave the conic hill no more ;
Surging flames, at last consenting,
　　Beat in vain the rocky door.

"Sits no more the swain, lamenting
　　Cities buried in the plain ;
Reeling Earthquakes groan repenting,
　　Neptune soothes the boiling main.
　　　　In the caves of Ocean sleep
　　　　Monsters of the placid Deep,
　　　　And the puny arm of man
　　　　Reins the huge Leviathan ;
Earth's green surface, renovated,
　　Feels the sovereign step of Men ;
Wolds no longer desecrated,
　　With the prowling robber's den.

" Distant tribes assimilated,
    Proud to cherish, not destroy;
Desert islands penetrated,
    With a warm, prolific joy.
        Field and flood, with all their sons,
        Widening as the river runs,
        Continents, as seasons roll,
        Peopled with the loftier soul,
Earth shall go, in light careering,
    Round the centre of her love,
Daughter of the stars, endearing,
    Beauteous to the suns above.

" And the viper disappearing,
    Exhalations slay no more,
Men may walk the earth unfearing,
    Pierce the forest, wind the shore.
        Man, the lord of time and tide,
        Talks across the Oceans wide,
        Lulls the rising storm to sleep,
        Puts his chains upon the Deep.
Grim disease malignant, failing,
    Flies before triumphant skill,
Powers of prudent life prevailing,
    Bloom upon the plain and hill.

" Dire malariæ cease exhaling,
    Man shall drive them from the land;
Genial airs, each sense regaling,
    Rise and breathe at man's command.
        · Time and space, elate to see
        Man's dominion wide and free,
        Load the breeze with joy and health,
        Load the fields with bounteous wealth.

Knowledge, o'er the nations flowing,
  Like the rivers, far and free,
Comes in countless streams, bestowing
  Hints from all the upper sea.

IX.

"Ye have been the hardy nurses,
  Toilers of the burning heart!
Ye have banished snares and curses,
  From the upward paths of Art.
    Charm the world from age to age,
    Gifted Poet, patriot Sage!
    Come the day, with starlit wing,
    Prophets rise once more, and sing!
Look, ye sons of aspiration,
  Toil has made your labors mild;
Toil hath snatched from desecration,
  Infant Genius in the wild.

"Toil hath rear'd your elevation,
  Paved the Hill which Science scales.
Fill'd the streets with animation,
  Fill'd with palaces the vales.
    Bless the hands that smooth'd the way
    Up to this celestial day!
    Hands that paved the world for you,
    Shall they share the glory due?
Heralds of the soul's progression,
  Lords of renovated earth,
Look adown the dark depression,
  See the cradle of your birth!

"O, the wondrous Intercession!
  Savage man escapes the curse;
Man asserts his new possession,
  Heirs his Father's universe!
    Lo! I scan the world to be,—
    Dædal Earth and Sapphire Sea
    From the dark, oblivious Fall,
    Man the rising lord of all.
    Shining on the azure height,
    Beauteous Ministers of light,
    Calling from the crystal sphere,—
    Mercy, Holiness appear;
And the lovely stars are greeting,
  Greeting mortals, as they roam,
Hearts of men and angels beating,
  Beating with the joy of home!"

X.

"Dear Ideal of the Graces!
  We have dream'd what you behold;
You, transcending times and spaces,
  See, as saw the Seers of old.
    See the habitable world,
    In a loftier Orbit whirl'd,
    Like a Bride adorned to meet
    ALPHA in the Golden Street.
Beaming Image of the morning,
  Thou must be a bride to-day:
See, the doves with gentle warning,
  Flitting o'er thee, soar away.

"Wondrous fair, without adorning,
  Lo! thy loving train attends,
Friends and guests, without suborning,
  All the Vale its beauty sends.
      EDWIN, see that son of mine!
      See his brow with rapture shine!
      Old am I, and worn with thought;
      Can this be a mortal's lot?
Long in loneliness repining,
  I become afraid of bliss!
Rapture fills me, past defining,
  Mountain, sky, one bright abyss!

"EDWIN, on thy arm reclining,
  Let me lean amid them all,—
All this convocation, shining
  In the light of Rosenhall!
      EARL OF MARSTON, WILLIAM bold,
      ORSON with a chain of gold,
      Rosy garlands, lilies fair,
      Load with redolence the air.
See! they crown the radiant Maiden,
  Round her neck the golden chain,
ORSON there with garlands laden,
  Tries to smile, but tries in vain.

"Hark! he calls her "Lulah Haden!"
  Kneeling reverent at her feet:
"Image blest of her in Aiden
  Keep me weeping till WE meet!"
      Thus he speaks,—and bending low,
      Tears in copious torrents flow;
      Mute Erasmus at her side,
      Holds the garlands for his bride.

Now the bridal vows are spoken,
  Kiss and golden signet given,
One, of mingling hearts the token,
  One, of endless love in Heaven.

"Fond, old Heart!—and still unbroken?
  Let me rest this reeling head!
Two immortals, wept, evoken,
  Coming from the grave to wed!
    And he sought her long in sorrow,
    Wept all night and watch'd for morrow,
    Died to ask the suns on high,
    Would they deign to make reply!
Just, when hope and reason fleeing,
  Did some Power mysterious fly,
Bear him through the vail of Being,
  Guide him through the open sky.

"Soul possesses in the SEEING,
  Here, the joy is to behold;
Ah! from clay vouchsafe the freeing,
  Let ME find one face of old!
    Once a maiden, blithe as Spring;
    Once she wore the bridal ring.
    Smiling with a mother's joy,
    Once she kissed her smiling boy.
Thus the world keeps blooming, fading,
  Oh! the rapture! Oh! the sting!
Streams of transport, torture, wading,
  Life, an endless wandering!"

Mid the garlands, round her braiding.
  Earl of MARSTON at her side.

On her ABINOS, unfading,
  Sits Elaine the blooming Bride
    All devoid of dread or fear,
    In her mountain mansion dear,
    Robed in spotless Sagamite,
    She more lustrous than the light:
She regained from bowers ethereal,
  Traveler of the starry blue:
She, who saw the Thrones Imperial,
  Saw the Right, the Good, the True.

Rose of Haden, majesterial,
  Sent to breathe her Wisdom here;
Voice, to sweeten pulse aerial,
  Heart, to ravish and endear;
    Love, our drink, and Faith, our food,
    Easy, joyful to be good.
    In the palace, in the wild,
    Shines a magic from the Mild.
In some lovely world of vision,
  Could our wicked feet abide,
Should we feel one base collision,
  Guilty thrill of lust or pride?

"Not frail insects of derision,
  Then to angels might we be;
Toys of passion, indecision,
  Trundling like a mop at sea.
    Framed was she a golden mean,
    Dwelling each extreme between,
    Image of Ideal joy;
    Naught can tarnish, naught decoy.

She beholds the base intention
  Hiding in the guilty brain,
Calms, at once each loud dissension,
  Banishes each sense of pain.

Knows your wish before you mention,
  Loves you with an angel's heart,
Hints the thought to bright Invention,
  Never claims herself a part.
    Image of the lucid Truth ;
    Stainless as the pastoral Ruth ;
    Could she speak a conscious lie,—
    She, sweet daughter of the sky ?
All the MARSTONS bend beside her,
  Hear her lips of music tell
Joys and fears that did betide her,
  Back to earth with Arrionel.

He, enthusiast, keeps the wider,
  Pondering how to deal with bliss ;
Should he hasten home, and hide her
  From a worrying world like this !
    Men have found it hard to know
    Pure, ecstatic love from woe ;
    Hope, fruition, if they meet,
    Bliss is pain, and hope, defeat ;
See ! his locks again, how glossy !
  Sparkling lustre in his glance,
Cheeks distended, blooming, bossy,
  Health, o'er all his countenance !

XI.

LIGHT—divine, that shines above us,
  In the blue abyss, so far :

Shining down, you seem to love us,
  Loving soul, and loving star!
    Living while the skies endure,
    Unapproachable and pure,
    Far, immaculate, serene
    Smiling all the leagues between.
Sacred in your consecration,
  Islands in a holy sea,
Glorious summits of Creation,
  Make us love your purity!

Pulses of the soul's elation,
  Thrill the intermundane tie,
And a holy approbation,
  Links us with the loving sky;
    Pure the dews and dewy flowers;
    Sacred homes and hearths of ours,
    Broods a heavenly spirit near,
    Spots with holy memories dear;
All the paths the wanderer traces,
  Have been trod by human feet,
Every land hath Holy Places,
  Shrines of History, Oh! how sweet!

Hand of stranger ne'er effaces
  Supersensual image there;
Dreamy forms, ideal graces,
  Make old weeds and winters fair.
    Something dearer than the day,
    Sinai, Horeb, Carmel, say,
    Whence exhales the fragrant wine,
    Holier than the Truth divine!
Spirit, white and pure reposes
  All around this earth of ours,

From the mountain side discloses,
   Grows among the classic flowers.

Flits through Idumæan bowers,
   Fragrance of the living soul ;
Lingering, breathing all the hours,
   O'er the Palm Groves, as we stroll.
      Ah! what living, beating heart,
      Smiled to meet, and wept to part?
      Righteous dictates of a will,
      Whisper in the zephyrs still ;
In the life of free volition,
   In the voice of truth and love,
Dwells the Holy Intuition,
   Beaming from the Life above.

And this charming apparition,
   Sweet, forgiving, pure Elaine,
Proves to earth a full fruition,
   Due to soul without a stain.
      See the blooming, joyous fair,
      Smiling rapture on the air,
      Garlanded with warm caressings,
      Clothed upon with nuptial blessings!
See a father's veneration
   Wept on her who could FORGIVE ;
Bright, divine impersonation,
   Showing how the world should live.

Hymen leads the Convocation,
   Sires, and sons, and damsels all,
Joyous in the glad Ovation,
   Banqueting in Rosenhall.

  Instruments of sweetest sound
  Echo from the walls around:
  Voices of the young and fair,
  Revel in the fragrant air.
Hopes and wishes, leaping, blooming,
  Flow upon the nimble tongue,
There, delicious sounds assuming,
  Ring the ambient lights among.

And the scented lights illuming,
  Tremble o'er the smiling face,
Holy amaranths perfuming,
  Seem to consecrate the place.
  Admiration, love inspire
  MARSTON with prophetic fire,
  Words in waving cadence flung,
  Words unbidden crowd his tongue;
  Now afar the sound is dying,
  Now symphonious chords replying,
  All to wondering ORSON seeming,
  Voice of Lulah, young and beaming;
Breathing love and sweet remission.
  From the low, incumbent sky;
ORSON, bent in deep contrition,
  Fills the pauses, sigh with sigh.

XII.

NYMPHAGION.

EARL MARSTON.

  Guests of the Bridal Hall.
  Praise to the God of all,
Praise to the Giver of banquet and cheer;

Join in the strain of love,
Sung in the light above,
Sung in the rapture of meetings so dear.
Praise to the beautiful,
Charming and dutiful.
Boon of my Lulah, and bride of the hour;
Sing of her purity,
Blooming maturity,
For SPIRIT is Holiness. Wisdom is power.

FIRST MAID.

Hues of the wilderness,
Lovely and limitless,
Each with a loveliness purely its own,
Stars of the Summer sky,
Each like a spirit-eye,
Watching the SOUL as she ponders alone:
Eloquent bond of us!
How they respond for us!
Those from the Solitude, these from ABOVE;
Hymen's implicity,
Blend all felicity,
And bless the two bosoms whose life is to love.

SECOND MAID.

Waving the yellow corn,
Cheerful the Summer morn,
Cheerful the minstrels in woodland and wold.
Smiling at Eventide,
Meadow and mountain side,
Shining so joyous in crimson and gold.
Oh! but our bonny Bride!
Ever the sunny side,

Beaming, resilient, from ringlet and brow,
    Always the bright of us,
    Beauty and light of us,
Can make all the past and the future shine now.

THIRD MAID.

    Gushes of happiness,
    Sudden and sorrowless,
Pass all around the gay Hall, at her will,
    Witty, with deference,
    Brilliant, with innocence,
She, like the Gipsy-Queen, dignified still:
    See how the Peasantry,
    Roar at her pleasantry,
Droppings of Paradise, fresh from the sky:
    Porter and ferryman,
    Master and merryman,
A laugh on the lip, and a tear in the eye.

WILLIAM.

    Who gave the Paragon,
    Mystic catholicon,
Skill to restore us from fracture and pain?
    Word of her rosy lip,
    Touch of her finger tip,
Sets the pale victim to smiling again!
    Deep in the history,
    Virtue, and mystery,
Plants of the forest and drugs of the mine,
    Finds this IDOTHEA,
    Instant Eumothea,
And fills all the mortal with vigor divine!

EDWIN.

Brightly the pebbles gleam
Under the flowing stream,
Crystal transparencies rippling away ;
Under the light of suns,
Health to the loving ones!
Purl their pure thoughts along, down in the day!
Artless sincerity,
Azure-eyed Verity,
Spread, like a sky, o'er the path as they go;
Honest simplicity,
Scorning mendicity,
Shall await them above, and endear them below.

REGENT OF ROSENHALL.

Hail to the happy youth,
Searcher of hidden Truth,
Honest and resolute, faithful and pure!
Moon of the vestal ray,
Sun of the golden day,
Shed your best rapture on loves so mature!
Free from all vanity,
Flowers of humanity,
Long may they bloom, to the Valley's delight!
Nature's Gentility,
Robed with humility,
Attuned to the pulses of Infinite Right!

ORSON.

Oh! ye shall hear of me,
Full words of honesty,
Me, the assassin of mother and child!

Rescued from Monsterhood,
Think of my gratitude,
Filled with proclivities generous and mild!
Think of my Cynosure,
Hopeful acclimature,
Toiling to die, with a prospect to live;
Living in sooth of it,
Infinite truth of it,
THE BEAUTY OF HOLINESS IS—TO FORGIVE.

FINIS.

AUTHOR'S NOTES.

"Idothea I," or, "The Beauty of Truth," was completed in 1884; "Good and Evil," in Idyls, was written, and extracts published at various periods, between 1840 and 1860; "Idothea III," or, "The Beauty of Holiness," was written since the last date. This possibly may account for want of uniformity in style and treatment.

The extracts from Æschylus, Sophocles, Euripides, Kotzebue, and Cramer are very free translations from the original Greek and German, but the stanzas under the title D'Holbach, are, of course, entirely original.

Notwithstanding great care in the typography, a few errors have escaped notice, in passing through the press. The reader will please make the following corrections: Page 136—second line of 2nd stanza from top, read "fiends" instead of "friends." Page 198, couplet at top should have followed line fifth from bottom of page 197. Page 216, "And the truth," —should be, "Let the truth," &c. On the following page, title to Idothea III, in Hebrew quotation, Ka-

DESHI should be KADESHIM, the last letter having casually slipped to the next word.

Occasionally the reader will discover the omission of periods at the end of sentences. This defect he will please supply. There are other typographical errors of not sufficient importance to demand special notice.

For the general reader it may be satisfactory to state that ALOMA is an epithet from the Indian dialect, signifying woody; ASSARIGOA was the name which some tribes gave to Virginia; ANDANUKEYAN or, AINDANUKEYAN, was applied by them to the whole country, and KADEAN, to the West.

I cannot consent to close these notes without recording, that the beautiful and pathetic lines, in Idyl I, under the name Musæus, were composed many years ago, by a very youthful and gifted friend of the author, and who is now a distinguished advocate and judge.

www.ingramcontent.com/pod-product-compliance
Lightning Source LLC
Chambersburg PA
CBHW022103230426

43672CB00008B/1262